The Streets of Key West

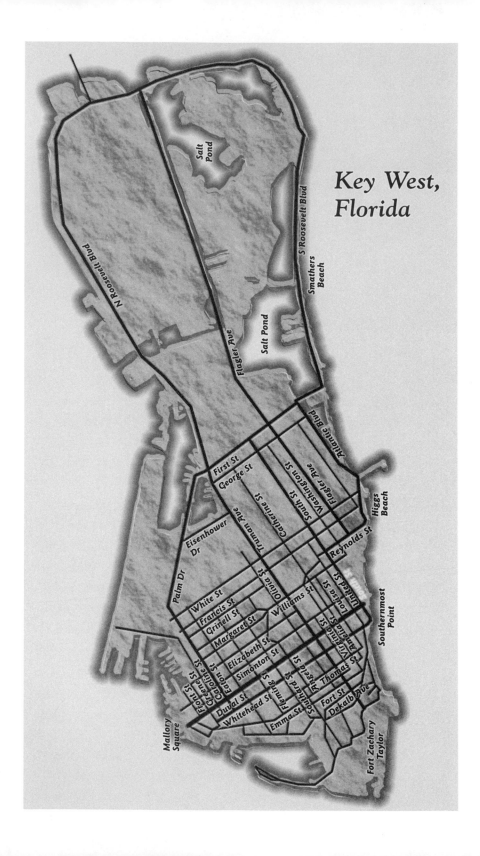

Key West, Florida

Salt Pond

Salt Pond

N Roosevelt Blvd

S Roosevelt Blvd

Smathers Beach

Flagler Ave

Atlantic Blvd

First St

George St

1 St

Washington Ave

Flagler Ave

Higgs Beach

Catherine St

South St

Eisenhower Dr

Truman Ave

Reynolds St

Palm Dr

White St

Olivia St

Williams St

United St

Southernmost Point

Francis St

Grinell St

Margaret St

Louisa St

Margaret St

Elizabeth St

Simonton St

Thomas St

Virginia St

Amelia St

Fort St

Dekalb Ave

Front St

Greene St

Caroline St

Eaton St

Duval St

Whitehead St

Fleming St

Southard St

Angela St

Emma St

Fort St

Mallory Square

Fort Zachary Taylor

The Streets of Key West

A History Through Street Names

J. Wills Burke

Pineapple Press, Inc
Sarasota, Florida

To Momma
and
In Loving Memory of
Daddy and Denny,
and
Mary Bernstein
Geography Teacher Extraordinaire,
and
Dr. Gene Tanzy
Writing Teacher Nonpareil

Inquiries should be addressed to:

Pineapple Press, Inc.
P.O. Box 3889
Sarasota, Florida 34230

www.pineapplepress.com

Library of Congress Cataloging-in-Publication Data

Burke, J. Wills, 1946-
  Streets of Key West : a history through street names / J. Wills Burke.— 1st ed.
      p. cm.
  Includes bibliographical references and index.
  ISBN 1-56164-317-3 (hb : alk. paper)
  1. Street names—Florida—Key West—History. 2. Streets—Florida—Key West—History. 3. Key West (Fla.)—History. I. Title.

F394.K4B87 2004
975.9'41—dc22

2004019100

First Edition
10 9 8 7 6 5 4 3 2 1

Design by Shé Heaton
Printed in the United States of America

Contents

Introduction

The streets tell the story—and what a story it has been. From a discovery of bones that gave rise to its name centuries ago, to today's modernity, Key West has had a long and colorful history. For the uninitiated, a stroll around *Margaritaville* is a pleasant enough experience; for those in the know, however, it becomes a cerebral delight during which the town's street signs whisper its secrets.

Like so many of you, I first arrived overland, across islands and islets, via causeway and bridge, a journey taken long after the island had been connected to the mainland. Upon arriving, I hardly noticed that I had crossed from Stock Island onto the key. I didn't feel that I was island-bound. I felt more like I had reached the tip of a long, narrow peninsula.

Key West was once a true island with no bridges to it, a

The sign starts the story.

coral outcropping marooned in subtropical waters. Known originally as *Guarugunbe* by the Indians, who used its south shore as grounds for the repose of their dead, Key West, by some accounts, served first as a funereal island. Other accounts paint a much darker picture, one of an Indian battleground, a killing field whereon the vanquished were left to nature's undertakers.

Whatever the case, bones there were—and waterlocked it was until centuries later when the key was connected to the American mainland by rail and road.

Spanish explorers were the first Europeans to set boot on the island. In the 1500s they landed and found it uninhabited, except for all those bones scattered about. They named their find *Cayo Hueso* (Bone Island), a moniker that would stick until the Conchs began arriving centuries later. Apparently they assumed that *hueso* translated to *west* in English. Cayo Hueso was, after all, the westernmost isle in the chain dubbed *Cayos de Los Martires* (Islands of the Martyrs) by the Spaniards.

Many of our common place names are similarly based on misunderstanding. Ironically, these misunderstandings lend an air of human fallibility, impregnate our names with even more meaning, and imbue them with a rich history. To wit, Columbus, en route to the East Indies in search of spices and other goods, thought that he had arrived when he made landfall in the Caribbean. Consequently he referred to the inhabitants of the islands as *Indians*, a name eventually extended to all aboriginal Americans.

So, place names are often erroneously derived. Indeed, the actual key west, the key farthest west, lies about sixty-five miles southwest of Key West and it is part of the Dry Tortugas: *Dry* apparently because of the lack of rainfall; *Tortugas* because their European discoverer, Ponce de León, noticed many turtles in the waters surrounding the islands.

When it was still a true island, Key West got its start because it was near the shipping lanes that coursed the Straits of Florida. The northwest sector of Key West, with its deep, protected harbor, was settled first. From here its history unfolded as its streets were laid out in a grid pattern that evolved eastward. From Front Street on the western waterfront to Roosevelt Boulevard and the remnants of Houseboat Row on its eastern edges, Key West has manifested its destiny in a unique manner, one that can be related by examining its street names.

Acknowledgments

Little that follows is original. Most has been gleaned from the books and magazines scattered about me, some from the Key West Memorial Sculpture Garden (where the idea for this project was conceived), and even more from various historic markers and signs that dot the most fascinating six square miles of America.

Special thanks go to Tom Hambright, scion of the Florida History section of the Monroe County Public Library, for sharing his knowledge of Key West's history and the origin of many of its street names. Other librarians were also helpful. Bob West, reference librarian at the Florida State Library, and James Cusick, curator of the P. K. Yonge Library of Florida History, located the maps that have been reproduced here, providing the best copies possible. Thanks also go to John Viele, the author and Keys historian who reviewed my manuscript. He made a number of useful suggestions and pointed out a couple of historical and geographical inaccuracies. His comments have helped to enrich the text and shape the book. Finally, I thank Nancy Frazier, the secretary at the City Planning Department, for sharing information about the origin of the names of some of the streets in her "New Town" neighborhood.

Nancy's warmth and willingness to befriend a stranger were indicative of the openness that greeted me in my search for

Acknowledgments

information. On my first foray I stumbled upon a lane I had not known existed. The gentleman sitting on the porch of his house (a former cigar factory cottage that straddles Higgs and Donkey Milk Lanes) paused from his activity and patiently told me how Donkey Milk Lane came upon so unlikely a moniker. And then there was the elderly lady taking her evening constitutional with her daughter. She didn't pause when asked if she knew how Newton Street came to be named, and I had to scurry behind to repeat my query and make out her throaty reply, "Sir Isaac. . . ." Indebted I am for her touch of levity.

But originality? I believe I can contribute at least one thing. Everything I read had placed Solares Hill at either Elizabeth and Windsor or William and Windsor (the site of Solares Hill Groceries). Standing at both locations, I could clearly see that one would still have to trek uphill to reach its eighteen-foot peak—which is near the Burton House on Angela Street, precisely twelve and a half steps from Whitmarsh Lane.

Now that I have made my contribution to the literature, it is all downhill in terms of originality. And downhill we go, down from the Burton House to Simonton Street, a most appropriate place to start.

At the end of our streets is sunrise;
at the end of our streets are spars;
at the end of our streets is sunset;
at the end of our streets are stars.
—George Sterling

Simonton Street

They lived in turbulent amity a couple of blocks from each other, Paul in a guesthouse on Simonton . . . and Billy in a small apartment on William Street.

—John Hersey, "Get Up, Sweet Slug-a-bed"

Even before John Simonton purchased the island from Spanish artillery officer Juan Salas, Key West had a colorful history. Aboriginal Americans (probably members of the Calusa tribe—but possibly their enemies) had left grim evidence that the island had been visited, if not inhabited. The presence of pirates was also evident to later visitors. Abandoned earthworks and freshwater wells, old coins, fragments of antiquated weaponry, and a gravestone etched in French bore silent testimony that others had been there much earlier than they.

And who were these later visitors, some of whom settled in for a longer stay? Prior to Simonton's purchase, the Keys alternated between Spanish, British, and American ownership. From Nassau in the British Bahamas seafarers were drawn to *Cayos de Los Martires*, known today as the Florida Keys, in search of mahogany for ship timbers, turtles for food, and shipwrecks for the bounty they might yield. Thus, in 1763, when Spain traded Florida to England (for Havana, which had been captured by the British), Bahamians were already familiar with *los cayos* and continued to visit Cayo Hueso. By then, the few Spanish families and the scores of Indian families who were residing on the island had relocated to Cuba.

By 1783 England, on the verge of losing its American colonies anyway, gave Florida back to the Spanish. Most of the Bahamian pioneers left the Keys, but a rugged, hardy lot (now known as Conchs for their ingenuous use of their namesake shell) stuck it out, and would eventually make their way to Cayo Hueso.

Thus was the state of affairs when, on August 26, 1815, Don Juan de Estrado, Spanish governor of Florida, granted Cayo Hueso to Juan Pablo Salas, an officer in the Royal Artillery Corps. Salas had not only rendered military service, he had also served admirably as postmaster and secretary to the colonial governor. At this juncture in their international adventures, the Spanish were strapped for cash, in part because of their involvement in costly colonial wars. By awarding his subject and servant a lonely, sparsely inhabited isle way down a chain of coral outcroppings topped by vegetation twisted like so many tortured martyrs, the Spanish governor helped balance the ledger by handily discharging his debt to Salas.

Salas did little with his domain—and probably for good reason. By 1819 Spain, still in need of cash, sold Florida to an adolescent United States. By July 1821 the territory had been formally transferred and incorporated into a nation manifesting its destiny in all directions. So, Cayo Hueso was no longer a part of Spain, and perhaps the trusting Spaniard began wondering whether his services had been compensated at all. In any event, Salas began covering his bases.

Enter John Simonton. A native of New Jersey, Simonton had wide-ranging business interests in Mobile, Alabama. A friend, John Whitehead, had advised him of the opportunity that Cayo Hueso presented: now that the Keys were a part of the U.S., this last link was well situated to become a major seaport. Simonton heeded the advice. On December 21, 1821, in Havana, for $2,000, Simonton agreed to buy the small island from Salas. On January 19, 1822, the deal was closed and Simonton took possession (or so he thought). Acting posthaste (out of distrust?), he caught the Gulf Stream to St. Augustine, where the transaction was recorded on January 23.

Soon after the purchase, Simonton sold an undivided quarter of the island to John Mountain (U.S. Commercial Agent/Havana) and U.S. Consul John Warner. The other quarters were sold to John Whitehead and John Fleming (spelled Fleming these days). Warner and Mountain did not hold their quarter for long. They sold it to Pardon C. Greene, who took up residence on the island.

At this point problems began cropping up. Salas, it seems,

was doing more than just covering his bases. He had also sold the island to John B. Strong, who in turn transferred his claim to yet another *John*, General John Geddes, former governor of South Carolina. Another Geddes (George) and a Dr. Montgomery led an invading force consisting of "two white carpenters and three negroes," according to the Honorable Jefferson B. Browne. They took possession of Key West in April 1822. How long the occupation force remained is not known. In any event—and in testimony to Simonton's clout and his Washington connections—the dispute was settled in his favor by a U.S. Land Claims Board on December 14, 1825. Thus began the quadripartite reign of Simonton, Whitehead, Greene, and Fleeming.

Cloud shadows raced down Simonton. Birds screeched and sang in the old Peggy Mills Garden across the street.

—Tom Corcoran, *The Mango Opera*

Simonton Street

Ernest Hemingway's first Key West residence was on Simonton Street. He and his family had left Paris, where they had been "very poor and very happy," and arrived (via steamer from Havana) in April 1928. They had intended to depart immediately by driving and ferrying over the newly opened highway that threaded its way to the mainland. Alas, their transport, a Model A Ford, was not available dockside as planned, so the dealer put Ernest and pregnant wife Pauline up in an apartment above his garage. Weeks later, during which time he resumed work on *A Farewell to Arms*, their car arrived, and Ernest bid farewell to Key West for the first time.

That first Hemingway domicile at **314 Simonton** has been modified into a stately building, the **Casa Antigua**. The Pelican Poop Shoppe has replaced the ground-floor garage.

Across the street and toward the Gulf, at the corner of Carolina, presides a solid, monumental structure that housed the post office and U.S. District Courthouse. Built in the Depression era, its exterior walls are made of coral slab quarried from Islamorada (so named by the Spanish for its purple beaches) in the Upper Keys. It is now the **Federal Building**, and district court is still held there.

Along the shore, on what used to be a waterfront lot between Duval and Simonton, Aeromarine Airways provided passenger and mail service to Havana in the early 1920s. By 1925 AA's flying boats (surplus World War I issue) were out of service, leaving a vacuum soon to be filled by Pan Am. Part of that lot is still vacant and home to 6400 square feet of sand that is known as the **Simonton Street Beach**. Across the way, where laborers once toiled in the Marine Railway Shipyard, tourists now lounge about in an upscale **Hyatt Hotel**.

Farther down Simonton, toward the Atlantic Ocean, the Sears School, Key West's first public school, was built in 1874. Demolished in 1909, **Free School Lane** marks its former location, but there are no other indications that the area had once been home to the island's first pupils. At the end of the lane, however, there is a sign that says **"Nancy's Secret Garden."**

Nancy's garden had once been the Peggy Mills Garden. Though Nancy claims that her acre is the only one left in Key

West that is in its original state, when Peggy acquired the property, it was anything but pristine. Only after tearing down the thirteen old dwellings that crowded the plot and then trucking in a ton of topsoil from the mainland did the site begin to acquire its current charm.

At **1100 Simonton** reigns a building that is hardly recognizable as a cigar factory. Built in 1920 after the original frame structure burned down years earlier, the Gato Cigar Factory eventually became U.S. government property. This concrete, fireproof building was used as a commissary by the Navy from 1950 to 1989. In 1998 it was gifted to the citizens of Monroe County, renovated, and transformed into today's office complex for the county and state.

I walked over to Simonton, past the old cigar factory, around the schoolyard and synagogue, and stopped at the lumber company.
—Thomas McGuane, *Panama*

Simonton's purchase, his dogged pursuit of his vision, and his eventual ownership of the island were pivotal in the development of Key West. Permanent settlement followed, and, in due course, the key was surveyed and mapped.

John Simonton became a snowbird, possibly Florida's first: winters in Key West, summers in Washington, where he exercised his clout on behalf of his winter home. A federal court was established on the island; a naval station opened; and army barracks and a marine hospital were built. Soon Key West became an official U.S. port of entry.

Bust of John Simonton, Key West Memorial Garden

While on the island, Simonton served as subtler of the port and representative for a New Orleans consortium interested in manufacturing salt. Upon leaving Key West, he moved to New Orleans, where he continued to engage in various business enterprises.

Simonton died in 1854. His daughter, Florida, inherited his holdings on an island profoundly shaped by his entrepreneurial spirit and stolid stewardship. Like her father, she had a keen sense of civic pride and duty. On June 21, 1871, Florida, through a trustee, deeded some of her holdings to the City of Key West, and for decades city hall sat on property that had been donated by John Simonton's heir.

Duval Street

She started turning up late at night drifting alone along Duval Street, protected by a serene beauty which scared off the usual needle-boy thugs and hot-rod Navy romeos cruising the bars for someone to write home about.

She was after the music. . . .

—Thomas Sanchez, *Mile Zero*

William Pope Duval was Florida's first territorial governor, and he would serve longer than any governor, territorial and otherwise, who would follow (April 17, 1822-April 24, 1834). Of French Huguenot forebears, he was born in Virginia in 1784. Young Duval set out for the frontier when he was only fourteen. He settled in Bardstown, Kentucky, where he read law and was admitted to the bar before his twentieth birthday. Within the next decade, he rode as a cavalry officer and served as a congressional representative (Kentucky, 1813–1815). Then, recommended by Secretary of State John C. Calhoun and appointed by President James Monroe, Duval came to Florida.

In St. Augustine he served as a territorial judge until 1822, when Monroe appointed him governor of the Florida territory. Though Florida now had a governor, it had no seat from which he could govern. As a compromise between the two most likely locations, Pensacola and St. Augustine, a state capital was chosen midway, near an Indian village called *Tallahassee* (*old fields* or *old town* in the vernacular). While awaiting the construction of the capitol, Duval governed from a boat docked at St. Marks twenty miles away on the Gulf of Mexico.

In a world dependent on water, wind, and current for commerce and transport, Gulf Coast ports played a vital role in the development of the South. Indeed, in the 1820s the United States was largely a cluster of seaboard towns, cities, and ports; the rest was frontier. Thus, as Simonton had divined, Key West was poised to take off. On a direct path between Europe and Mexico, Cuba and Gulf Coast ports, and en route (via the Straits of Florida and the Gulf Stream) to the East Coast, Key West was well positioned to serve as grand chandler for ships passing by.

Duval, however, is remembered more for the attention he gave to internal affairs. There was an "Indian problem" to be dealt with. Upon signing a treaty in 1823, the Seminoles agreed to relocate to a large tract of land south of Lake Okeechobee. The Indians in and around the capital departed peaceably enough, but they did not like where they were sent. (One problem was that it had no access to the Gulf or the St. Johns

River.) Duval, perhaps skeptical of the secretary of war's assurance that "they will acquiesce without trouble," went south to inspect their reserve. Finding the best of their land to be worth little, Duval estimated that "nineteen twentieths . . . is by far the poorest and most miserable region I ever beheld." Consequently, he recommended that they be relocated to more arable land, but the Seminoles were mistrusting. Eventually the Seminole Wars, some of the bloodiest fighting ever seen on American soil, broke out and lasted for decades.

A true Renaissance man, Duval struck up friendships with the literati of his time, some of whom wrote stories containing characters molded on him. Washington Irving characterized him in "Ralph Ringwood," while a lesser-known but much more widely quoted writer, Irving's in-law James Paulding, based "Nimrod Wildlife" on the former Kentucky frontiersman. Paulding is the author of that much-repeated, tongue-twisting ditty about Peter Piper picking pecks of pickled peppers.

Consuela's grandfather . . . used to tell her about having gone as a boy to the all-Cuban school in the upstairs rooms of the ornate San Carlos Institute on Duval by day and being taken to Cuban musicals downstairs in the evenings.
—John Hersey, "The Two Lives of Consuela Castanon"

Duval Street

El Instituto de San Carlos, which formerly stood at **516 Duval Street**, was named for the saint for whom Carlos Manuel de

Cespedes was christened. Carlos, a wealthy Cuban plantation owner, was a patriot whose cry *Cuba Libre* sparked the Ten Years' War, an ill-fated revolt against Spanish rule. Founded by Cuban political exiles in 1871, the institute served as a venue for Cuban culture, revolutionary politics, and socializing. Financed by profits from Key West's burgeoning cigar industry, the institute has been destroyed and rebuilt a number of times.

The current structure at 516 Duval Street, now called the **San Carlos Opera House**, designed by Cuban architect Francisco Centurion y Maceo and built in 1924, is an ornate and formidable example of Cuban architecture. In need of a place to carry out its consular functions, the Cuban government purchased the site and funded the construction. The new building also served as a social club, school, and auditorium. The Cuban government still owns the property and building.

Farther down Duval, in the **1100 block**, stands another monument to Cuban independence. The trendy restaurant **La Te Da** now occupies the building where Cuban patriot José Martí spoke to cheering crowds from the second-floor balcony of Teodoro Perez's family home. Following his visits that helped unify the island's fractured independence movement, the house was christened *La Terraza de Marti* in his honor. Lawyer, poet, statesman, and revolutionary, Martí (1853–1895) was killed in his homeland, at Dos Rios, while leading a revolt against the Spaniards.

Back toward the Gulf stand a couple of buildings of historic interest. Both the **Old Customs House** and the **Oldest House** were moved to their present locations from nearby. These relocations were facilitated by the construction of many old buildings well off the ground. A common practice during the settle-

The La Te Da. José Martí spoke here.

ment of Key West, the elevation of buildings allowed high tides and storm surges to pass beneath the structures.

The first **Customs House** (circa 1876), now at **124 Duval**, was originally located on Front Street. There, between 1876 and 1888, it served as an entry point into the U.S. and a location where salvagers could officially declare goods taken off reef-stranded wrecks. Imported Cuban cigars were also cleared there.

The **Oldest House, 322 Duval Street,** was built in 1829 by grocer Richard Cussans. Captain Francis Watlington, a prosperous salvager (or wrecker), purchased it in the 1840s and moved it to its present location, where it now houses the **Wrecker's Museum**. Watlington, also a customs inspector and harbor

St. Paul's Episcopal Church, named for the patron saint of shipwrecked souls.
It once faced the harbor.

pilot, served as a lieutenant in the Confederate Navy. His grave can be found in the Key West City Cemetery, near Clara and Fourth Avenue.

At the **corner of Eaton and Duval** stands **St. Paul's Episcopal Church** (so named for the patron saint of shipwrecked souls). Earlier structures facing Eaton were destroyed repeatedly (hurricane in 1846, fire in 1886, and another hurricane in 1909).

Sometime after the last disaster, church fathers decided to change the direction of St. Paul's so that it faced Duval. The upshot of this reconstruction and relocation is that John Fleeming, the only one of the island's original owners to be buried on Key West, is now interred under the foundation of the church. When the church was rotated so that its entrance faced Duval, its graveyard became entombed beneath the sanctuary. The former rectory, however, an original structure not destroyed by the 1909 hurricane, still stands where it was first constructed.

Eaton and Duval must have been church central. The first Roman Catholic Church (1852) was also located nearby. St. Mary, Star of the Sea, Church was destroyed in a 1901 fire and subsequently relocated to what is now Truman Avenue.

A couple of decades later, the seven-story **La Concha** was built a block away at **430 Duval Street**. In its early days the hotel served many a sojourner awaiting the ferry to Havana or arriving from Cuba after their ninety-mile journey. Considered a high rise on the island, it was the first thing on Key West that Hemingway saw. Its dominance of the skyline caught his attention when he steamed in from Havana for the first time. Drab and colorless in those days, the La Concha, which was called the Key West Colonial for a few years in the 1930s, was splen-

Established in the 1920s, an enduring Key West landmark.

didly refurbished by the Holiday Inn chain. In recent years, the Holiday Inn sold its landmark property to Crown Plaza Hotel–Resorts.

Then they came to the edge of the stream and the water quit being blue and . . . I could see . . . the wireless masts at Key West and the La Concha up high out of all the low houses . . .
—Ernest Hemingway, *To Have and Have Not*

At the **far end of Duval**, near South Beach, presides the **Southernmost Mansion**. Casa Cayo Hueso was built by Judge J. Vining Harris at the turn of the century and owned by his fam-

Southernmost Mansion, one of Judge J.V. Harris's legacies.

ily until 1939, when the Ramos-Lopez family purchased it. For years this family, whose ancestors migrated to Key West from colonial St. Augustine in 1819, used the estate as their private residence. Only recently has this monument to Queen Anne architecture been converted into a museum replete with Hemingway and other Key West memorabilia.

. . . he slipped away from the bustle and glare of Duval Street, its carnival vapors of candy and grease, and disappeared into quiet residential precincts where cats slunk through lattice under porches, and household shadows sent mysterious patterns through the slats of louvered windows.

—Laurence Shames, *Virgin Heat*

Whitehead Street

Through the crystal-clear air Lori could hear the ringing of the agent's bell . . . that had begun when the packet had first been sighted, carefully picking its way past the outer reefs toward the lighthouse at Whitehead's Point.

— Thelma Strabel, *Reap the Wild Wind*

John and William Adee Whitehead had an impact on Key West that went far beyond their years spent there.

In many respects, the modern-day story of Key West begins, fittingly, with a shipwreck. In 1819, en route to Mobile from New York, John's vessel foundered off the Bahamian coast. Onward passage was arranged on a ship that made port at Key

17

West. Whitehead was impressed by the potential that the island's harbor held as an entrepôt for passing vessels. As indicated earlier, he passed his impressions on to fellow business-man John Simonton, who acknowledged his gratitude by cutting Whitehead in on ownership of the key.

John Whitehead's Key West years were but a brief interlude in an active life. Following the lead of his father, William Sr., John spent his early years as a clerk in Newark banking circles. Eventually he entered the mercantile business in New York. There he demonstrated the grit, independence, and risk-taking that characterized the brothers Whitehead. He organized a business partnership and struck out for Mobile on the northern coast of the Gulf of Mexico.

John lived on Key West for eight years. Self-employed at first, he became a partner in the firm of P. C. Greene and Company (1824–1827). After the partnership was dissolved, Whitehead continued his residence, intermittently, until 1832. He then relocated to New Orleans, whence he established him-self as an insurance agent before moving on to New York. He returned to Key West only once. A lifelong bachelor, John, accompanied by a nephew (William's son), came back for a visit during the Civil War, in 1861. He died the next year.

William Adee Whitehead, John's younger brother, spent ten very active years on Key West. These were years spent in projects that indelibly shaped the Key West that we see today.

William was born in 1810, in Newark, New Jersey. He attended Newark Academy until he was eleven years old. This was his only formal education. Eight years later we find him in Key West, surveying, mapping, and platting that distant, sparse-ly inhabited island. The "Whitehead Plat" of 1829 set the town boundaries and (continuing the pattern set by the isle's first surveyor, H. L. Barnum) laid out the streets in typical grid fashion. Whitehead also platted the land in a manner that divided real estate equally among the four owners. Although one of the streets (Anderson) named during the first mapping has disappeared, all others remain, their monikers intact.

By the next year, William was appointed collector of customs for the Port of Key West, a post he would hold until June 1838. In March of 1831 he proposed a resolution to the town council (to which he had been elected) that called for it to procure the permanent services of an Episcopal minister, one who would be required to stay on the island and open a school. The resolution passed, the minister arrived (now William would no longer have to conduct funeral services!), and Key West's first school opened in 1834. In October of that year our Renaissance man branched out into newspaper work: he became the chief editorial writer for the newly established *Enquirer*.

William Whitehead had the foresight to preserve copies of his newspaper and its predecessor, the *Key West Gazette*. Many years later (1869), he sent these bound volumes to the Monroe County clerk for preservation. We are also indebted to William for his early chronicling of Key West's history. His account, written in the 1830s, provided the springboard for Walter Maloney's more thorough rendition on July 4, 1876. (In turn, the Honorable Jefferson B. Browne made generous use of Maloney's Centennial Address in his 1912 expansion, *Key West: The Old and The New*.)

William Whitehead continued his ascent. He ran for office and was elected to be Key West's third mayor—but, in performing his duties, he had a crisis of conscience that led to his leaving the island forever.

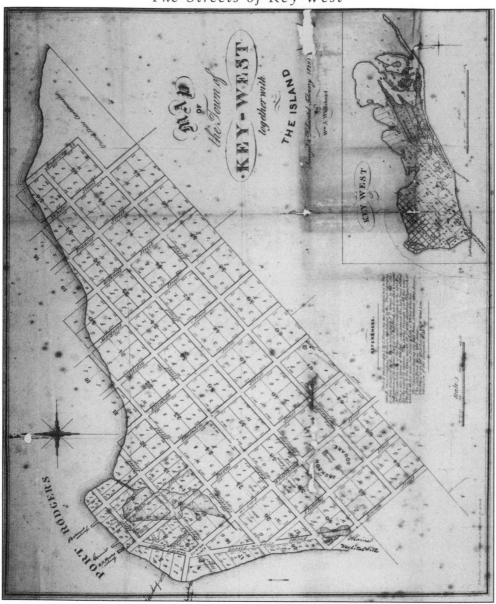

Whitehead's 1829 Map. Note how the blocks are divided into quarters,
one section for each of the four founders. (See page 4.)

The city charter of 1836 specified that an occupational tax be levied. A number of the town's fathers objected to this revenue-enhancing measure and refused to pay. Whitehead felt duty-bound to carry out the dictates of the charter. He requested that the city council call a town meeting "to determine whether the laws shall be enforced or the charter dissolved." The council refused. Whitehead called a snap election and announced that the winner could succeed him. Soon after the election he left Key West, never to return. Only twenty-eight years old, he moved back East, where he launched another multifaceted career. He died in 1884.

If Whitehead Street continued another ninety miles, instead of ending abruptly at the sharp edge of the Atlantic Ocean, St. Cloud could keep right on going until he walked down the palm-lined avenues of Havana.

—Thomas Sanchez, *Mile Zero*

Whitehead Street

Whitehead was the first street to stretch from the Gulf to the Atlantic, or, more technically, from Key West Harbor to Hawk Channel, beyond which run the Straits of Florida. William Whitehead's 1829 map shows the road reaching clear across the island, but this was no doubt more plan than realization. Browne indicates that virtually the entire key was still in a natural state until late into the 1830s. Probably at the time of the mapping the streets did not extend far beyond the confines of the population (some 300) clustered near the port. An 1832 sketch shows Simonton, Duval, and Whitehead (streets that form the spine of the island) ending at Olivia. Apparently Whitehead's grid simply overlaid everything, even the large tidal pond that entered near Greene and Front, crossed Simonton, straddled Duval, and edged Whitehead.

The large back yard sloped down to The Pond, the wide, shallow tidal basin that was crossed by a narrow foot bridge—the continuation of Duval Street.

—Thelma Strabel, *Reap the Wild Wind*

Whitehead's imprint went beyond his macro grid of the streets. The lots he platted off the streets were of slender dimension (46 feet by 90 feet). Ship's carpenters then built houses with little regard for the location of existing units on neighboring plats. To compound the "problem," paths and alleys angled off the streets where convenient and entered lots at varying intervals. Thus we have the whimsical hodgepodge that gives Old Town its funky charm of today.

At **1 Whitehead**, at harbor's edge, sits the **Key West Aquarium**, a monument to both innovation and desperation. Built by the Emergency Relief Administration (ERA) during the Depression, this tropical, open-air aquarium was the first of its kind anywhere and Key West's first tourist attraction. Inside, on walls that hold built-in tanks, can be seen Depression-era murals painted by artists commissioned by the ERA.

A few blocks from the aquarium, on **Whitehead at**

Caroline, stand the **Presidential Gates**, so dubbed since Harry Truman made Key West his southern getaway. Previously an entrance to the Key West Naval Base, these iron gates and pilasters were in place early in the century, long before they provided the ceremonial entrance to the President's Little White House.

Truman nods to Smith, accepting the adjournment, and reporters surge up . . . and scramble off towards the annex gate of Whitehead Street, racing to the phones.

               —John Hersey, "A Little Paperwork"

Nearby, at the **corner of Fleming**, close to the Monroe County Courthouse, U.S. 1 begins (or ends). Starting at this point, **mile zero**, a string of mile markers ends at Mile Marker 126 in Florida City on the mainland.

Stretching up the Eastern Seaboard of the country to Ft. Kent, Maine, U.S. 1 marks the start of our national system of highways. Odd-numbered U.S. highways run north-south and end on U.S. 101 along the Pacific Coast. Even numbers start in the North and run east-west, ending with U.S. 98 along the Gulf Coast. (The Interstate System simply reverses this numbering pattern.) Thus, Key West provides the cornerstone for a system that crisscrosses the nation, an honor celebrated beneath a magnificent kapok tree at the "End of the Rainbow" —and the beginning of "unlimited opportunities."

. . . he'd migrated around the country according to the weather. . . .
called it "packing the tepee and following the buffalo." He always
made it back to ground zero, at Mile Zero.

—Tom Corcoran, *Gumbo Limbo*

Farther down, at **704 Whitehead,** is the stately **AME Zion Church** (Cornish Chapel). Established in 1865 by freed slaves, it was originally called the First African Methodist Episcopal Church. Its current structure dates from 1894.

The **Key West Lighthouse** (1847) stands tall on the **900 block of Whitehead.** One of Florida's first, it was originally fifty-eight feet high and close to the water. Over the years it was elevated to seventy-eight feet so that its beacon could be seen above the sprouting trees. Since its erection, dredge-and-fill operations have expanded Key West considerably, and its land area has more than doubled in size, placing the lighthouse so far inland that it now appears to be an anomaly.

Now landlocked.

Continuing along Whitehead (while U.S. 1 veers north on Truman toward the mainland and onward to Ft. Kent, Maine) we reach land's end: what was once the Southernmost Point of the entire United States. Like Key West, however, the U.S. has also expanded, and, like the lighthouse, the concrete nun buoy (a replica of a channel marker three times as large but much more buoyant) that marks the spot is also an anomaly. Now the Southernmost Point in Key West has surrendered its former distinction to Ka Lae (South Cape) on the big island of Hawaii.

In 1851 Connecticut Yankee Asa Tift carved out a home from subterranean coral rock at what is now **907 Whitehead**. His two-story Spanish Colonial mansion, replete with the island's only basement, graced a spacious acre on Whitehead. Eighty years later Pauline and Ernest Hemingway purchased it for $8,000.

Favorite niece Pauline had been favored once again. The same uncle (Gus) who gave the Hemingways that Model A Ford for a wedding present gave Pauline the money for the house. As you may recall, the Ford's absence dockside precipitated their first stay, which apparently piqued Ernest's interest in Key West. Did this later gift also influence the Fates?

Ernest Hemingway was an American expatriate. Until he moved to 907 Whitehead, all of his adulthood had been spent abroad. After he left Key West, he lived for twenty years in Cuba before repatriating briefly—tragically briefly. So, until the very end, Key West was the only American locale that the adult Hemingway resided in. Was it coincidental that the city he chose was as far as possible from mainstream America?

Hemingway wrote only one novel set in America, *To Have and Have Not*. While living in Key West, he wrote about Key

Hemingway's house at 907 Whitehead.

West, a town hardly representative of mainstream America. Here we find a man, an artist, living and writing on the literal edge of his native culture.

How might Ernest's Key West years figure in his rise and fall? Hemingway was an early master of the art of self-promotion. Carefully crafting his persona into an image of manliness, he became Papa, the American patriarch; *Bwana* Hemingway, the great white hunter; and Hem, the hard-drinking, skirt-chasing man's man. This image took hold and grew in Key West. Did image turn into self? And then, when that self could no longer live up to the fabrication. . . .

Whitehead Street

In the old days he would not have worried, but the fighting part of him was tired now. . . Colt or Smith and Wesson . . . admirable American instruments so easily carried, so sure of effect, so well designed to end the American dream. . . .

—Ernest Hemingway, *To Have and Have Not*

From the street you can no longer see much of the house that Tift built and Hemingway immortalized. In 1937 a wall, made of bricks scrounged from Duval Street when the island's first sewage system went in, was erected to assure the writer's privacy. Vegetation also obscures the view, but less so now that Hurricane Georges has felled a huge banyan tree in the side yard. Now you can see Hemingway's second-floor writing studio from Olivia, the side street bordering the property.

But, for the price of admission, you can see it all. And after the tour you can linger about the grounds and revisit the mansion if you wish. Browse the bookstore, gaze upon the writer's studio at your leisure. You can even take another tour and let your imagination roam back to another era, back to when Papa and Pauline and son Patrick and baby Gregory were under the same roof.

Thomas, Emma, William, Margaret, and Caroline Streets

These streets were named for the siblings of John Whitehead. We have already met William, but regrettably we won't be meeting the others. There is no record or mention of them, so presumably they never walked the streets they were named after.

Thomas and Emma Streets

Thomas and Emma Streets run parallel to Whitehead, toward the Atlantic side of the island. Together with a stretch of Whitehead that roughly parallels the truncated Thomas, these three streets form the soul of what was once called Jungle Town, *La Africa*, or, as indicated in the *Mile Zero* quote, more pejorative names. Most recently, someone has come up with the safe, sanitized, theme-park-friendly name **Bahama Village** to

Thomas, Emma, William, Margaret, and Caroline
designate an area that reflects so much of Key West's rich mix
of race, culture, and language.

*. . . a place marked on the early Key West maps as Africa Town.
A place still called Nigger Town, Black Town, Tan Town, or
home, depending on the color of one's skin.*
—Thomas Sanchez, *Mile Zero*

Hemingway went regularly to the boxing matches at the
Key West Arena next to the old Blue Heaven Billiard Parlor at
Thomas and Petronia. Sometimes he refereed; at times he
fought; but mostly he watched. He and a heterogeneous mix of
islanders watched prize fighters, mostly black, who provided
inexpensive entertainment during the Great Depression. The
establishment that is now there goes by the same moniker, **Blue
Heaven**, but you'll no longer be able to shoot pool. The main
building has been converted into an art gallery, and a smaller,
separate building is now the base for a full-service restaurant
that serves its fare alfresco.

*. . . and across, behind the hotel, to the street that led to jungle
town, the big unpainted frame house with lights and the girls in the
doorway.*
—Ernest Hemingway, *To Have and Have Not*

La Africa was originally inhabited by a mix of Bahamians and Cubans of varying African descent. With them came their religion, their music, and their sport. Catholicism coexisted and often commingled with Santeria. Jazz great "Fats" Navarro came of age on Thomas Street. More affluent Conchs, wealthy Cubans, and city politicians would park their cars on Emma and proceed on foot to join the hoi polloi at the cock fights in the open-air arena off Amelia Street.

Today, shotgun houses and cottages, yesteryear's domiciles for the cigar rollers, still crowd narrow lanes and alleys, and *grocerias de madres y padres* still sit cheek-by-jowl with houses of worship that seem to have edged out houses of lesser repute. But you'd better see it now, before Bahama Village is restored and gentrified beyond recognition.

We drove into a section of town that real-estate brokers and black entrepreneurs call Bahama Village. It was the last repository of island tradition that had not been remodeled and resold.

—Tom Corcoran, *Octopus Alibi*

William and Margaret Streets
Walking from the foot of William to the foot of Margaret, among all the shrimp boats driven in by heavy weather, some with the net spilled . . . and others with the net streaming gauzily from the boom, various sea animals stranded in the web. . . .

—Thomas McGuane, *Ninety-Two in the Shade*

Thomas, Emma, William, Margaret, and Caroline

This pair of siblings resides in a more affluent part of Key West. On the other side of Simonton now, toward the Gulf (but snubbing Elizabeth for the moment), we come upon William and then Margaret.

At the foot of Margaret, at water's edge, near the docks, once sat the island's first turtle cannery, built in 1849. At its peak, when A. Granday's Canning Company was operating at this location in the early 1900s, the industry was bringing in some four hundred green turtles a day from as far away as the Nicaraguan coast. Once corralled, they were eventually processed into a daily average of two hundred quarts of "Fine Green Turtle Soup," a world-renowned delicacy. Parts of the turtle not processed for export were consumed locally. Where Granday's once ground out its product now sits a more convivial establishment, the **Turtle Kraals Restaurant and Bar** at **1 Land's End Village**.

Four hundred turtles a day, at two to four hundred pounds a pop, added up to a lot of turtle to be warehoused before being turned into soup. While awaiting the abattoir, they were housed seaside in turtle kraals, Spanish for *corrals* (though one source cites Afrikaans for *pens*). Notwithstanding the Aquarium's claim of being Key West's first tourist attraction, turtle death row may have antedated it. In the 1930s the kraals were dubbed Turtle Farm, and 15 cents was charged to view the ill-fated creatures. The attraction of yesteryear has been replaced by the **Turtle Kraals Museum, 200 Margaret Street**.

Margaret never sang here.

This was how Joe Coe came to Key West, to sell his skiff load of prizes from the sea of plenty, fresh brimming baskets of turtle eggs and live she-turtles, their pierced front and back flippers tied through with palm thatch.

—Thomas Sanchez, *Mile Zero*

Proceeding away from the docks in the bight, you will, no doubt, note that Margaret dead-ends at the **Key West City Cemetery**. It starts again at Truman, at the site of the cleverly named **Margaret-Truman Launderette**.

William Street approaches the cemetery before being turned into Windsor at the **Solares Hill Groceries**. On this stretch of William (a shorter stretch is on the other side of the island) stand some houses of historic and architectural interest.

In the **300 block**, next to each other, are the **John Curry**

Near the summit, elevation 18 feet.

and **George A.T. Roberts Houses**. This Curry House (there are others) is a story and a half high. Built in the early 1840s, it may not be the oldest on the island, but by Key West standards, it is ancient. Its neighbor, the George Roberts House (again, there are others of this same surname) was built by the Roberts who was cigar-maker-turned-merchant. Decked out in ornate gingerbread trim, the Roberts House is another fine example of Queen Anne architecture.

Nearby are two of Key West's **Bahama Houses**. Like its sister on Eaton Street, the one at **408 William** (also called the **Richard Roberts House**) was originally constructed in the Bahamas (Green Turtle Key), dismantled, and shipped to Key West for reassembly. Toward the end of this stretch, at **643 William**, across from the Cuban *groceria*, stands yet another Roberts house. The **Edward Roberts Eyebrow House** (circa 1880) gives us a glimpse of what has been described as an "architectural eccentricity." Windows have been fitted up high, dropped just beneath the eaves, for shade and to capture the sea breeze and efficiently circulate air within.

Marcelline's house is on the dead end of William Street, what was the dead end until the fire department opened it on through for access to the wooden tinderbox houses of this old quarter . . . so that what was once still as countryside now carried the tin murmur of Truman Avenue.

—Thomas McGuane, *Panama*

Caroline Street

. . . another hurricane hit from the northeast. One house, at the corner of William and Caroline Streets, was washed to sea with a male servant still inside.

—Burt Hirschfeld, *Key West*

Caroline Street, once the inland boundary of fledgling Key West, starts at the stately **Presidential Gates** on Whitehead. There, Whitehead begets Caroline, who then cuts an elegant swath past founder Simonton and siblings William and Margaret. She stops at Grinnell, perhaps affronted by the ill-kept grounds of the old **City Electric plant**.

Pauline Hemingway, who remained in Key West after she and Papa divorced, once worked on Caroline Street. She bought a spacious two-story structure at **525 Caroline** and went into the drapery and upholstery business with family friend Lorine Thompson. (Ernest used the Thompson Docks at the foot of Caroline and often fished with Lorine's husband,

Charles.) Pauline died in 1951. When consoled by fellow writer Tennessee Williams, Hemingway dug down for another of his "true sentences": "She died like everyone else and after that she was dead."

For the past few years Pauline's place has been home to the **Caroline Street Clinic** and the headquarters of **Captain Outrageous**.

Nearby, at **529**, the brick **Arapian House** stands out among its wooden neighbors. Edward J. Arapian, an Armenian, was born in Turkey, educated in Paris, and enriched in Key West. Sponge trader extraordinaire, he built his home, with its tin roof, turret, and trim, in 1906.

On the next block stand a few noteworthy places. Dr. J. Y. Porter, to whom we will pay a longer visit later, lived out his life (literally) at **429 Caroline**. He died in the same room in which he was born! Across the street, at **410**, is the **George Carey House**. Built by the Brit in 1834, it was expanded after Carey married in 1844. In 1934 Jessie Porter Newton, the good doctor's daughter, bought the house and cottage out back. Poet Robert Frost was a frequent cottage guest.

Toward the end of **Caroline**, at **901**, is one of the newest additions to historic tourism on the island. **Flagler Station**, a Historeum, Museum, and Gift Shop, celebrates what was once touted as the Eighth Wonder of the World, the Overseas Railroad, which stretched from the mainland to a spot near the station.

Greene and Elizabeth Streets

On the blank white wall on both sides of the door of Universal Cleaners, on Elizabeth Street . . . there are twin paintings of big white-footed black cats, facing each other, maternally licking the faces of their kittens. . . .

—John Hersey, "The Wedding Dress"

Walter C. Maloney, in his historical sketch written for Key West's centennial celebration, indicated that Elizabeth was "some relative of Mr. Greene." No other information about this relative is available.

Of Pardon C. Greene, we know much more. Born in Rhode Island in 1781, he found his calling at sea. He was the master of a merchant vessel that sailed between Cuba and U.S. ports along the Atlantic Coast. Thus, he became familiar with Key West and, as related earlier, seized the opportunity to share in its ownership. His family did not join him; they remained in Rhode Island.

So, who was this mysterious relative whose importance in Greene's life merited the naming of a street after her? A favorite niece? A kissing cousin? Did she live on Key West?

Or is the street really named after a relative of another of the island's original owners? Fleeming's mother-in-law, Elizabeth Rodman Rotch, did, after all, help him purchase his quarter of the island.

In any event, we have an Elizabeth Street that fits nicely between Simonton and William, thus filling in all the streets between sisters Emma and Margaret.

Elizabeth Street

The most prominent feature on Elizabeth is the black-and-

Gently clean to purrfection.

After being whitewashed, the mural was lovingly restored by Jackie.

white mural that captures your attention as you slip out the side exit of the **public library**. The painting, so aptly described by Hersey, frames the entrance and covers much of the storefront. For a time, while the laundry itself was being gently cleaned, the mural was whitewashed to oblivion. But now, thanks to Jackie, whose signature can be found next to the diminutive cat on the north side of the building, the mother cats are back to their gentle cleaning.

Farther down, away from the Gulf, at **620 Elizabeth** is the former residence of bottler Douglas T. Sweeney. He was already producing soda water elsewhere on the island when he constructed a bottle factory on Simonton. Cutting his commute to a stroll, Sweeney built his residence facing Elizabeth, back to back with his workplace.

Less than a block away, at **702**, is the **Merrill-Jackson Cottage**, former residence of poet James Merrill and his literary, lifelong partner. The cottage is another of the island homes that were constructed in the Bahamas, disassembled and transported, and then put back together on Key West (theirs about 1840). Its photograph graces the cover of Lynn Kaufelt's *Key West Writers and Their Houses*.

Greene Street

On the harborside end of the island, Elizabeth intersects Greene. Not far from here, at the waterfront, once stood "Greene's wharf." In the early years, this wharf and neighboring warehouse were the only prominent structures on the island.

Pardon C. Greene was quite prominent in Key West. He headed up P. C. Greene and Company; attended the first service at St. Paul's Episcopal on Christmas Day, 1832; and enrolled as a charter member the next day. He also served the city briefly as mayor. Unlike Sweeney, Greene elected to separate work and home: his residence was at the other end of his namesake street, at its corner with Whitehead, the present-day site of the **Audubon House**. Greene died in the autumn if 1838. His only child, William, died at Ft. Jefferson (Dry Tortugas) in October 1860.

Greene Street figures prominently in Hemingway lore. Soon after the repeal of Prohibition in 1933, Joseph "Josie" Russell moved his small speakeasy, **Sloppy Joe's**, to a more spacious establishment (The Blind Pig) on Greene. Good friend and fellow fisherman Ernest Hemingway, a man who had a way with words, convinced Josie to restore the original name, Sloppy Joe's. There, in December 1936, a blond siren dressed in black sashayed into Sloppy Joe's and caught Papa's wandering

Site of the second Sloppy Joe's, where Ernest met Martha.

Papa drank here.

eye. Foreign correspondent Martha Gelhorn was destined to become the third Mrs. Hemingway. But the Fates were unkind: their marriage was his shortest.

Soon after their fated meeting, **Sloppy Joe's** moved down the block. Josie had been renting from Isaac Wolkowsky for $3 a week. Wolkowsky demanded a dollar a week more; Josie balked —and then acted quickly. Deciding that it was better to own than rent, he purchased the Victoria Restaurant building at the **corner of Duval and Greene** for $2,000. The new establishment was just half a block away, so Josie recruited his regulars to move bar, booze, and bar furniture into the new location. Paying in trade, he opened that night.

The old telegraph office was located on Greene, near the second Sloppy Joe's, which is now **Captain Tony's**. In 1867 the International Ocean Telegraph Company (IOTC) laid cable that linked Cuba and Key West. By 1872 IOTC had purchased the brick building at the **corner of Telegraph Alley** that became the focal point of world attention in 1898. At this site, news of the sinking of the U.S.S. *Maine* in Havana Harbor was first received and subsequently disseminated worldwide. Soon Key West became a staging area for many journalists hankering to cover the Cuban campaign of the Spanish-American War. These days **416 Greene** is home to the **Emerald Lady**, a nicely appointed jewelry store that graces the corner.

A few years before the war, another brick building, **City Hall**, was built on Greene Street, on land deeded to the city by John Simonton's daughter, Florida. The more solid structure replaced a two-story frame structure that burned ten years after its dedication on July 4, 1876, the Centennial of the Declaration of American Independence. Indeed, the fire of

41

1886 not only destroyed City Hall, it also devastated the key's business area and took out a few docks.

Fires were common in nineteenth-century Key West. During that centennial celebration, a fire broke out soon after civic leader Walter C. Maloney began giving his "concise" history of Key West (from a small, 1820s waterfront settlement to Florida's largest and most prosperous city in 1876). The crowd dispersed, never to return, and Maloney's oration (which would have lasted three hours!) was never finished. Consequently he decided to have the sixty-eight-page speech printed. So, some of the island's property may have been lost on America's hundredth birthday, but a great deal of its history was preserved.

It may be stated here. . . that the streets, other than those bearing their own names, were designated by the proprietors in a way to perpetuate the names of relatives and personal friends. Anderson *was so called after the name of the then Comptroller of the Treasury;* Eaton *after the Secretary of War;* White *after the Territorial Delegate in Congress;* Duval *after the Governor;* Grinnell *after the merchant of that name in New York;* Southard *after the Senator and Secretary of the Navy;* Caroline, Margaret, William, Thomas, *and* Emma, *after the brothers and sisters of John Whitehead;* Frances *after a daughter of Mr. Fleeming;* Ann *after Mr. Simonton's wife;* Elizabeth *after some relative of Mr. Greene;* Fitzpatrick *after Richard Fitzpatrick a then resident. . . .*

—Walter C. Maloney, A *Sketch of the History of Key West*

Front Street

---

*Jack Roberts owned a sandwich shop on Front Street [serving] sand-
wiches, soup of the day and a green salad, key lime pie. . . .*
                    —Burt Hirschfeld, *Key West*

riginating as a path near water's
edge, Front Street was probably the island's first street. That
Walter Maloney's history of Key West did not mention it is
understandable. This street did not meet his criteria for inclu-
sion, and its naming is obvious. Fronting the harbor, it runs
along the waterfront.

Originally, Front began just north of Simonton, ran the
length of the deepwater harbor, and ended near the intersection
of Emma and Fleming.

Before rail and road linked Key West to the mainland, the sea was its life link and Front Street the interface between it and the islanders. The wharves (Browne's Tift's, Greene's, Filer's, and Simonton's) were nearby; fishermen, salvagers, and spongers put to sea here; and seagoing vessels took on precious provisions at sundry ships' chandlers along the front.

Located on Front Street, near its **intersection with Greene**, is the latest incarnation of the old **Customs House and Post Office**, a stately, multistory brick building that used to dominate the waterfront. A splendid rendition of Richardson Romanesque architecture, it was built in 1891, in plenty of time for a U.S. Court of Inquiry established to investigate the sinking of the *Maine* to convene there in 1898. Now landlocked (bounded by the Hilton Hotel and its car park), this imposing building is currently home to the **Key West Museum of Art and History**. Around back, on the Key West Aquarium side, squats an old cistern.

In 1852 the U.S. Navy established its headquarters along the harbor, north of where the Customs House is today. Now all that remains of what was once Navy property is **Building No. 1 at 291 Front Street**. Until 1932 it was used exclusively by the Navy, first for coal storage and later for administrative purposes. From 1932 to 1939, the U.S. Lighthouse Service ran its Key West operation out of the building. The U.S. Coast Guard was the last of our sea services to work out of what has become the oldest brick structure on the key. The Guard's tenure ended in 1977. Since then private enterprises (currently **Island Specialty Shops)** have taken up leases at this historic site.

During its heyday, the U.S. Navy also expanded south and enveloped Front Street, leveling houses, Mallory's Coconut

Customs House and Post Office, 1891.

Harborside view of Customs House and Post Office, 1891.

Grove place included, in its wake. Now the former naval station and its annexations are in private hands. Owned by Pritam Singh, it has been aptly dubbed the Truman Annex, for this is where Truman's **Little White House** is located.

Sailors are renown for enjoying their liberty, and Front Street served as their "entertainment central" long before Duval earned that dubious distinction. But more legitimate establishments, like the Havana-Madrid Club (formerly at the terminus of Duval at Front), shared the strip with joints of baser standards, one of which was Papa's favorite.

Across from where the club was located was the First National Bank. Founded in 1891 and known for years as the First Union Bank, it was recently acquired by **Wachovia** and splendidly renovated. Back when it was still First National, this triangular-shaped building figured in more of the island's Hemingway lore.

By the time Ernest returned to Key West to live, he had long finished the book he was working on in the flat above the garage on Simonton. Flush with royalty checks from *A Farewell to Arms*, he tried to cash one at the First National Bank. It seems that the First National was a bank of high standards, though. Established in 1891, after the collapse of the bank of Key West, it didn't cater to just anyone, especially an ill-kempt stranger. Bank President William Porter refused to cash Hemingway's $1,000 check, so Hem stopped in the first speakeasy he saw, a tiny place on Front called Sloppy Joe's. Proprietor Joseph "Josie" Russell promptly cashed the check and won a lifelong friend and customer. As we have seen, when liquor became legal again in 1933, Josie relocated to the Blind Pig on Greene Street.

Front Street

Formerly the First National Bank, 1891, where Hem couldn't get a royalty check cashed.

So Skelton slipped into their garage and got his fishing rod, walked half a block to the corner of Front to the Dos Amigos bar . . . and shot one maladroit game of eight-ball with counter-revolutionary Cuban shrimper. . . .

—Thomas McGuane, *Ninety-Two in the Shade*

Eaton Street

On Eaton Street, trying to sneak, I dropped about a gram on the sidewalk. I knelt with my red and white straw and snorted it off the concrete. . . .

—Thomas McGuane, *Panama*

Eaton Street is named for John H. Eaton, U.S. senator (Tennessee), secretary of war, territorial governor of Florida, American minister to Spain, and biographer of President Andrew Jackson.

Eaton succeeded William Duval to become Florida's second territorial governor. Arriving seven months after his appointment, he served but two undistinguished years (April 1834–March 1836). His prior appointment, however, as secretary of war in Jackson's Cabinet, was far more consequential and tumultuous. Ironically, the difficulties he encountered in

Washington had their origins in St. Marks, not twenty miles from Tallahassee, where he served as governor.

In 1817 General Andrew Jackson led an expedition to the Florida frontier. He had been sent there to prevent the massacre of American settlers by Indians. Ignoring instructions to await further orders, Jackson plunged into Spanish territory, captured the fort at San Marcos, and summarily executed two Brits for espionage. A considerable diplomatic upheaval followed, and Secretary of War John C. Calhoun called for Jackson to be censured for "exceeding his orders." Thus was born a lifelong enmity between the two that would ensnare the Eatons some fourteen years later.

Fast forward to 1831: Jackson, well into the third year of his first term as president, had been criticized from the onset for his cabinet choices, only one of which (not Eaton) was deemed "prominent." Critics charged that Jackson was a despot, that he relied exclusively on cronies outside his cabinet (hence the origin of the term, "kitchen cabinet"). One such critic was arch-enemy Calhoun, who had become Jackson's vice president. (At that time, president and vice president did not run as a pair on the same party ticket.)

Class politics may then have reared its snobbish snout. A clique of conservative cabinet wives led by Mrs. Calhoun refused "to recognize" the high-spirited Peggy O'Neil Eaton. Fellow Tennessean Jackson backed the Eatons, but, caught up in the turmoil, Secretary Eaton relinquished his office. Total reorganization of the much-criticized cabinet ensued, and the Eatons were eventually exiled to Tallahassee.

So, why was a street in Key West named for John Eaton? It could not have been because of his short term as governor of territorial Florida. (The street was named years before he served.) And why would Key West's Founding Four name a street for a fledgling secretary of war from Tennessee? An obscure entry in a three-page, unpublished document simply titled *Key West Streets* may hold the key: "Named for Sne. [sic] John H. Eaton Pres. Jackson's Secretary of War and later Governor of Florida 1834–35. He owned property on Whitehead in 1829."

Was Senator Eaton a Key West property owner as indicated above? Could his property have been located near where Eaton now intersects Whitehead? We may never know for sure.

Eaton Street

A block over, beyond the corner of Eaton and Whitehead, there is plenty of evidence to explain why the Cubans dubbed Eaton *Calle Iglesia* (Church Street). As indicated earlier, St. Paul's originally faced Eaton (and one could still visit founder Fleeming's grave). Not far from St. Paul's stands the **Old Stone Methodist Church** at **600 Eaton.** Built of quarried stone in 1877, it is the oldest religious edifice on Key West.

A bit farther northeast, at **712,** stands the **Peacon/Calvin Klein/Octagon House** (so named for its builder, former owner, and eight-sided second-floor veranda). A bit of its real estate history reveals recent trends in property prices. In 1974 interior decorator Angelo Donghia bought the house for $45,000; six years later he sold it to clothes horse Calvin Klein for a cool 975K, overpriced (for then), but still clearly indicative of the market. (In the summer of 1998, shotgun fix-'er-uppers were going for $169,999.)

On the next block, at **730 Eaton,** is one of the Bahama

Houses. Following the destruction caused by the hurricane of 1846, lumber and other building materials were in great demand on the island because so much had to be reconstructed. Rather than compete for the scarce resources, Joseph Bartlum and brother-in-law Richard Roberts (whose home we visited at the other Bahama House, **408 William Street**) set sail for Green Turtle Cay. There they painstakingly dismantled a couple of houses and floated them back to Key West. Bartlum also purchased a neighboring lot (**718 Eaton**), where daughter Rosella and her husband built a house joined together without nails or bolts, but with plenty of wooden pegs.

Enduring Echeverria's asinine play-by-play of every person walking down Eaton. Old ladies. Gays. Men with their dogs.
—James W. Hall, Red Sky at Night

Fleming Street

A trickle of breeze. . .stirring the oak limbs and making the shadows jitter on the pavement of Fleming Street . . .
 —James W. Hall, *Red Sky at Night*

John W. C. Fleeming was born in England in 1781 and taken to the United States at a tender age. Like John Whitehead, Fleeming was in the mercantile business in Mobile, Alabama, a friend of John Simonton, and one of the original owners of Key West.

Early in 1822 Fleeming, Whitehead, and U.S. Consul Warner landed on Key West to take stock of their island. By year's end Fleeming had left the cay for New Bedford, Massachusetts, where he married Mary Rotch, his stepfather's niece. He did not return to Key West until 1832.

Apparently his primary interest in returning was the development of a salt manufacturing industry on the island. No dabbler in this endeavor, Fleming had gone to Europe where he learned about the production of sea salt. His *El Dorado* was to have been the natural salt ponds that covered an even larger section of the island than they do today. His untimely death later in 1832, however, put an end to this dream and everything else.

Fleming's widow, Mary, arranged his burial in the churchyard of St. Paul's Episcopal Church. This property must have been part of Fleming's share of the island; in May of 1838 Mary deeded a two-hundred-foot-long tract of land along Eaton to the vestry of St. Paul's. Months later construction began on a more permanent church, one built of native coral rock. It was near completion when destroyed by the 1846 hurricane (that also uprooted the cemetery between town and Whitehead's Point on the northeastern side of the key).

John and Mary Rotch Fleming had one daughter, Caroline. Notwithstanding Maloney's clear indication that Caroline Street was named for a sister of the Whitehead brothers, some speculate that it was really named after Miss Fleming. Similarly, some maintain that Frances Street (soon to be trod upon) was originally Francis, named for step-dad Francis Rotch, who took Fleming to the U.S. with him when little Johnny was a child. And what of Elizabeth and William Streets? Is there also a Rotch connection? Were they named for father-in-law William and mother-in-law Elizabeth? Given that Fleming actually married his step-cousin (Francis Rotch's niece), this is all rather baffling. But can't you just see the Founding Fathers, huddled over their pints of port, naming streets for multiple personalities—and delighting at the confusion dazed researchers would face centuries later?

Whatever the case, we know for sure that Fleming Street, even with an *e* dropped, was named for John Fleeming. Let us see what there is of interest along this, the last of our streets named for the original proprietors.

Fleming Street

Not far from St. Paul's is **Fausto's Food Palace**. The original, the island's oldest mom-and-pop grocery, is elsewhere on Key West. Is this one on Fleming Street the second link in an expanding chain?

Next door, at **532 Fleming**, is the building that once housed the key's first private hospital. Dr. John Bartlum Maloney, a grandson of W. C. Maloney (the author of *A Sketch of the History of Key West, Florida*), was a surgeon for the Florida East Coast Railroad. In 1908, as rail was being laid down the keys, there was an explosion on Big Coppitt, and the survivors were taken to Key West for treatment. Maloney converted his office on Fleming into a hospital to meet the emergency. It remained a hospital and was named for his helpmeet, Louise. Years later, John bought the Sawyer residence at 504 Simonton Street. The back of his new home was adjacent to the hospital, so, for the sake of convenience, he connected home and business with a ramp. Like his grandfather, John fulfilled his civic duty by serving a term or two as mayor of Key West.

At the **corner of Fleming and Elizabeth** is the **Monroe County Public Library**, where many an afternoon was spent digging out the information presented here. Books were well regarded on the island long before Hemingway set up shop on Simonton. In April 1892 the Key West Library Association was established; on September 15, 1892, South Florida's first public library opened in the Masonic Temple. Decades later, in 1915, the Key West Women's Club took the lead in providing library services for the island. Through the club's fundraising efforts, the current library was built. It opened in November 1959.

The Sparks Chapel Methodist Church, named in honor of first pastor J. O. A. Sparks, was located at the **corner of Fleming and William Streets.** Toppled by the hurricane of 1908, its replacement, the more prosaically named **Fleming Street Methodist Church,** now graces the corner.

A few blocks down, **at Fleming and Margaret,** is the site of an old sponge warehouse where the sea harvest was stored during the industry's short-lived revival. (With the assistance of the Civil Works Administration, sponging resurfaced during the Depression era, but never regained prominence as a principal industry.) For years the building housed Perkins and Sons

The only clue that the sponge warehouse was once at 901 Fleming.

Chandlery. Now it is home to **Signs and Designs**, a commercial art enterprise. The only indication of its former uses is up high, beneath the apex of its roof. There, in splendid bas-relief, a mermaid, decked out in her aqua pastels, keeps a steady vestigial watch over her former domain.

Now, toward the end of the street, we come upon the **Eden House**. Built in 1924 and first named the Overseas Hotel, this hotel once housed railroad workers. Perhaps it was this blue-collar ambience that attracted hippie hoards to this haven in the late 1960s and '70s. Goldie Hawn and company also found its ambiance pleasing. They filmed the movie *Criss Cross* there.

Finally, we arrive at the early home of the Hemingways' friends, Charles and Lorine Thompson. The house at **1029 Fleming**, built in 1867 by grandfather Thomas T. Thompson, was home to the couple in the 1930s.

Southard Street

He'd driven those many miles without any terminal mechanical trouble, but on Southard Street in Key West the brake drum had had enough and caught fire.

—Thomas McGuane, Ninety-Two in the Shade

Samuel L. Southard (1787–1842) was both a governor and a senator in New Jersey, secretary of the Navy, and an interim secretary of both war and the treasury. Probably his public service in New Jersey was the reason a street in southernmost Florida was named for him. (As noted, the Whitehead family hailed from Newark.) It is, however, his national public service that is of most interest.

As secretary of the Navy in the John Quincy Adams administration, Southard incurred the wrath of Andrew Jackson during Old Hickory's bid to become our seventh president. Southard had the temerity to state, not just suggest, that

"Mr. Monroe and not General Jackson was entitled to the credit for the victory at New Orleans." Southard claimed that Jackson had more or less abandoned his army and was returning home prior to the famous battle for the Crescent City when Secretary of War James Monroe ordered him back to his post. Not heeding the counsel of the ever-present Eaton, Jackson had words directly with the secretary. Southard, backpedaling quickly now, assured Jackson that no deprecation was intended, that his exploits "form a part of our national glory," which Southard never meant to tarnish. Southard was branded a "consummate ass" by the Democrats and lost his job as secretary of the Navy after Jackson became president in 1829.

Southard Street was called *Calle Curteles* (Barracks Street) by the Spanish-speaking islanders. *Calle Curteles* was the route between the entrance to Ft. Zachary Taylor on one side of the island and the Army barracks on the other. Let's see what is of interest between these two points.

Southard Street

At the **corner of Simonton** still stands the **Southern Bell Telephone Company** building, looking the same as it did about 1915, when it was built. From within, four operators would route calls from their state-of-the-art switchboards, while, outside, line crews on horse-drawn wagons stood ready to repair.

Blocks away, at the **corner of Margaret**, presides a building that many a Key Wester passed through. In 1909 Harris High School replaced the Sears School; by 1924 another high school had been built, and Harris High became Harris Elementary. The stately building and its grounds are still being put to public use. General Equivalency Degree (GED) classes and other

A mom-and-pop store. No sisters?

community-service activities are held within. The Monroe Association of Retarded Citizens (MARC) is also located there. A nursery where clients can learn horticulture skills graces the surroundings.

At **Southard and Grinnell**, we have a corner *groceria*. The **5 Brothers Grocery and Sandwich Shop** can't be missed. A group portrait of the brothers graces the balustrade above the entrance.

At **620 Southard** is the **Lowe House**, so named for sponge and lumber entrepreneur John Lowe Jr., who owned Key West's first sawmill. In the 1930s it was the residence of Dr. Julius Stone, the director of the Florida Emergency Relief Administration (WPA).

On Southard, in front of 5 Brothers Grocery, two middle-aged men cursed and shouted. Accusations, denials, revised accusations. A down-and-dirty lovers' spat.

—Tom Corcoran, Gumbo Limbo

Fitzpatrick Street

Fitzpatrick, a short block wedged between Front and Greene Streets, is named for Richard Fitzpatrick, who was, as indicted by Maloney, "a then resident." In fact, Fitzpatrick was one of the island's first residents. In the spring of 1819, when he was thirty years old, Fitzpatrick emigrated from South Carolina.

An entrepreneur with diverse interests, he was the only authorized auctioneer of salvaged goods on the island in the 1820s. Then, in 1830, Fitzpatrick became the first of many who attempted to manufacture salt from the ponds in the southeast sector of the key. He leased the Whitehead portion of the salt ponds, hired some thirty hands, and even used his political pull to bolster his position. It was all for naught: in 1834 he abandoned the effort. His bid to build Key West's first jail (stone, with cistern) met a similar fate when John Simonton underbid him for the job.

As a politician, the Honorable R. Fitzpatrick fared better. He served for years as a Monroe County delegate to the Florida

Territorial Council, and in 1836 was chosen to be council president. It was while he was a delegate that Fitzpatrick used his power to further his business interests. When the council introduced a measure to establish the North American Salt Company on the island, he blocked passage of a bill that would have brought the corporation there. This precipitated an animosity toward him that may have played a role in his relocating to the tip of the mainland.

Whatever the reason, in the 1830s Fitzpatrick bought two thousand five hundred acres of what is now very prime real estate and built a vast plantation along the banks of the Miami River. Again, he was fated to fail. In 1835 war broke out between the U.S. and the Seminole Nation, and he had to abandon the enterprise. By 1842, when hostilities were temporarily halted, his holdings were in ruins.

Later that decade, his nephew, William E. English, acquired the land and platted the Village of Miami on the south bank of the river. English fared no better than his uncle, however. While chasing another fortune in the California Gold Rush, this Forty-niner accidentally shot and killed himself. His dream of developing south Florida was left to others to realize.

Fitzpatrick Street is home to **Kino Sandals**, a family enterprise established in 1966. You can still get a decent pair of slip-ons at a reasonable price in this specialty shop located in the corner of the street's only open-air arcade.

Tonight she wore a white hibiscus-flowered cotton that matched her red Kino sandals and the scarlet blossoms she had tucked into her ash brown hair.

—Dorothy Francis, *Conch Shell Murder*

Ann Street

The Civil War came and they built two blockade runners for the rebellion. . . . At what is now the foot of Ann Street, they built a series of deadly blockade boats, light, fast, and armed.
—Thomas McGuane, *Panama*

Ann Street, as indicated by Maloney, was named after Ann Simonton, John's wife. Presumably she accompanied him while he wintered in Key West; no doubt, she was hostess to many a Washington fete during which John influenced D.C. lawmakers on behalf of the island he partly owned.

Ann, not as short a street as Fitzpatrick, covers two blocks between Front and Caroline. In the late 1800s, the Cortes Company located its three-story cigar factory there. Until it was demolished by the 1910 hurricane, Key West's brick firehouse was also on Ann Street, behind City Hall.

During the late 1970s and early 1980s, biographer Joseph Lash (the Roosevelts, Winston Churchill, Helen Keller) and wife Trude spent winters in a rented cottage at **217** (the **Ann Street Compound**). Nearby (and what on Ann St. isn't?), at **123-125**, Tom McGuane and family lived in a couple of conjoined shotgun houses while he was writing *The Bushwacked Piano*.

Key West, a clapboard town accreted upon a marine hummock at the end of the continental shelf, seemed a peculiar place to have buried Clovis.

—Thomas McGuane, *The Bushwacked Piano*

Grinnell Street

Let's sit by and very quietly watch as they gather for a game . . . in Forester's living room, in his modest converted conch house in a compound on Grinnell Street.

> —John Hersey, "A Game of Anagrams"

Grinnell Street, broken only by the plotting of the City Cemetery in 1847, stretches across the island. For more than a century this street has played host to a couple of enterprises that add to the island's history.

At roughly midpoint between the waters that bracket the island, at the **corner of Catherine**, squats a two-story building that used to be the **Armas de Oro Cigar Factory**. Of the hundred or so factories that once housed rollers, packers, and their readers (who helped break the tedium by reading to the workers), this structure is one of the few that remain. Its latest incarnation speaks to both our bounty and our propensity to accumulate stuff. It is now the **Old Town Self Storage** depot.

On the other side of the cemetery, Garfunkel's, a sprawling men's clothing and furniture store, once dominated the entire corner of Fleming and Grinnell. (In the early 1900s, Garfunkel and other Jewish merchants relocated to that emerging village, Miami.) Finally, at the foot of Grinnell, there was more evidence of government-assisted economic revival. In 1933 the Civil Works Administration, in hope of resuscitating a once thriving industry, built sponge docks there.

There is little more of historic interest along this mainly residential street. So, do we cite Maloney (who says the "Grinnell" is after the merchants of that name in New York), mention that they may have financed Fleeming's purchase of his share of the island, and move on? Or is there more to these mercantile Grinnells?

At the time the street was named, there were three Grinnell brothers, all born in New Bedford, all engaged in the family shipping business in New York. Joseph, the eldest, would outlive (1788–1885!) brothers Henry and Moses, but all were long-lived and, no doubt, accomplished much during their three score and more. It is, however, Henry who captures our attention here.

More deserving of a full-scale biography than the few paragraphs that follow, Henry Grinnell (1799–1874), businessman, philanthropist, founder of the American Geographical and Statistical Society, and financier of far-reaching expeditions, was in the vanguard of nineteenth-century exploration. Thus, it is with some irony that a street was named for him in what was then the most tropical of all American cities, for his interests were entirely in the opposite direction.

By the middle of the nineteenth century, only two unexplored areas of the world remained: the interior of the "dark" continent and the polar regions. So far no Key West connection to Central Africa has been uncovered, but Henry Grinnell provides a direct link to the North Pole.

Grinnell financed two Arctic expeditions between 1850 and 1855 that were launched in search of British explorer Sir John Franklin, who disappeared while searching for that elusive Northwest Passage to the East. The Grinnell expeditions did not succeed in finding Franklin or evidence of his demise (that would have to wait until the 1930s), but their search did result in the exploration of many Arctic lands. Thus we have Grinnell Peninsula jutting northwest off Devon island, Grinnell Land on Ellesmere Island, and Grinnell Glacier near Frobisher Bay. And, of course, we have a street on a semitropical island never visited by the Grinnell for whom it was named.

There is nothing worth living for but to have one's name inscribed on the Arctic chart.

—Alfred Lord Tennyson

Frances Street

. . . and cut around the cemetery. I put some effort into it, getting up speed, blowing through pools of vermilion petal under the Poinciana trees on Frances.

—Tom Corcoran, *The Mango Opera*

Depending on the source, the street that runs between Truman and James Streets is of either masculine or feminine origin. Maloney's 1876 paragraphs on street origins leans toward the feminine version (named after **Frances**, a daughter of founder Fleeming), while Jameson cites a masculine Fleeming connection. He says that the street was named for **Francis** Rotch, Fleeming's step-dad. (As mentioned earlier, these Fleeming-Rotch-New Bedford connections do keep popping up.)

Whatever its origin, Frances/Francis is not only androgynous; it also appears to be quite ecumenical. Skirting the **City Cemetery**, it edges both Jewish and Catholic plots. Other than this, the street's only claim to historic fame is at **609 Frances**. Constructed in 1886 by Bahamian master builder John T. Sawyer, this **Sawyer House** is an architectural gem. But rarely is anything on Key West left alone. An early twentieth-century hexagonal addition gives the structure its Key West funkiness: quirky and slapdash, yet somehow blending well with more classical design.

I went over to Francis Street for bolos and coffee and was taken aside, right on the sidewalk, by a man who wanted to know if I had any angles on local attics. He was a collector . . . of barbed wire and Orange Crush bottles.

—Thomas McGuane, *Panama*

White Street

hite Street is so named for Colonel Joseph M. White, an early Florida territorial delegate to the U.S. Congress. A Key West resident and property owner (part of Square 39, Lot 2 on Whitehead St.), White was the principal proponent of establishing a hospital on the island.

Probably collaborating with the influential Simonton, in 1836 White introduced a congressional resolution that called for the construction of a U.S. Marine Hospital on Key West. Seamen were forever getting scurvy and they often tried to cure themselves by eating citrus products, thus we have the term "limey" for an English sailor. Sitting astride the Straits of Florida and thus a hub for shipping in the Gulf of Mexico, Key West was the logical place to treat them. So, Representative White proposed a hospital "not only for our seamen, but for those navigating vessels (trading with) St. Marks, Apalachicola, New Orleans. . . ."

By 1844 the **Marine Hospital**, designed by Robert Mills, who was the architect of the Washington Monument and the Smithsonian Institution, was constructed right at water's edge, its entrance easily accessible by boat. Landlubbers could enter from **Emma Street**. The Marine Hospital operated until 1943 and still stands, but these days it is part of the larger **Mills Place**, a collection of condominiums that includes the renovated hospital. It is located within the grounds of the old Navy Yard, which is now the splendidly appointed **Truman Annex**.

But now let's go back across town, to where White Street makes its humble beginning Gulfside, near the Key West City Electric stacks. **Across from Peary Court** is the old **National Guard Armory**. Built by the same Sawyer we just met on Frances Street, the armory's twin towers once stood sentinel over a city park. Now residents of the Navy housing development there have one of the better landlocked views on the island.

Nearby, at **624**, is the **Elizabeth Bishop House**, home to the poet. Purchased in 1938, it was sold a decade later on the condition that it remain as is. It has, eyebrow windows and all, the only apparent addition being a *Friends of Libraries U.S.A.* plaque that graces the front gate and says

> *Should we have stayed home*
> *Wherever that may be?*
> —Elizabeth Bishop

At the **corner of White and Truman** stands a building that, like a few remaining others, was once home to the island's thriving cigar industry and now houses the **Green Tara Yoga Studio.** Here devotees practice Bikram yoga, a choreography of poses performed in an overheated environment. A flyer on the door invited me to a "Shamanic Dreamy Workshop," in which a dream guide would help me explore possible future realities. Another yoga studio with coffee shop is nearby, over on Watson.

Farther down, on the Atlantic side at **1105 White**, is the first **Fausto's Food Palace**, originally named Gulfstream.

Bikram yoga, the latest incarnation at this renovated cigar factory.

She grinned and turned down White Street in time to see Skelton's father streak into the alley past the Gulfstream Market.

— Thomas McGuane, *Ninety-Two in the Shade*

On White, **between United and Seminary**, presides what was formerly Key West's second high school. Built in 1924 and prosaically named Monroe County High School, it replaced Harris High. Then it became Glynn Archer Junior High when a portion of the salt ponds was filled in to accommodate yet another new high school. Most recently, the former high school has been turned into an elementary school.

It had been years since Fausto's bought Gulfstream Market, but it's still strange to see that sign on White Street.

— Tom Corcoran, *Bone Island Mambo*

At the **end of White Street** is the **Charles "Sonny" McCoy Indigenous Park**. Named in honor of the former mayor of Key West, current Monroe County commissioner, and perennial history buff, this area serves as a bird sanctuary and native tree haven. McCoy has become a living legend in the Lower Keys. Besides holding the record for serving the most consecutive terms as mayor (five), he lays claim to another endurance feat that still stands. On September 10, 1978, Mayor McCoy waterskied from Key West Harbor to Havana Harbor in six hours, ten minutes.

Also at the **end of White**, but **on Atlantic Boulevard** near the pier and to the left of the AIDS Memorial as you face seaward, is the **Southern Gateway**, a linear park replete with twisting trail and tangled native vegetation. This gateway stretches some two hundred meters and anchors the southern extremity of the East Coast Greenway, a long-distance trail that connects all major cities along the eastern seaboard of the U.S. Farther down Atlantic Boulevard is the **Key West Nature Preserve**. Broken by a large, exclusive residential compound, this expanse of natural vegetation has been made accessible by a couple of boardwalks that lead to the sea. Along the way, interpretive signs inform us of the different varieties of mangrove, buttonwoods, and other flora native to these wetlands.

Finally, in graceful counterpoise, rests the **AIDS Memorial**. Imbedded beside the concrete walkway onto the **White Street Pier**, rectangular slabs of polished granite, one inscribed with names of the departed, silently echo the anguish and memories of the survivors.

The sky is blank but beautiful,
Nothing will ever be the same—
A cup of emptiness to fill
Symbols shaped into a name.

—Rachel Hadas, "The Bees of the Invisible"

AIDS Memorial. Remembrance of lives past.

Anderson Street

The captain of our watch is stationed at our barracks, but this is way out Carolina Street way, beyond Elizabeth.
                    —Thelma Strabel, *Reap the Wild Wind*

Those of you familiar with Key West know that there is no Anderson Street on the island. As Maloney indicated, indeed there *was* an Anderson Street, and it was named for Joseph Anderson, comptroller of the treasury—but it wasn't there for long. Running parallel to White, Anderson was the street closest to the water on the north side of the island. By 1832 it had simply disappeared when the U.S. Army expanded its cantonment and built barracks where the street had been.

So, what was there is no longer; much of what replaced it is also gone, and the terra firma we tread upon today was sea muck and water at the turn of the century. Dredged up from the sea, compacted and given names, it forms part of the created land mass that has doubled the island's size in one hundred and fifty years. But before we see what uses have been made of this area, let's get a glimpse the life of the man whose name first designated this reach of the island.

Anderson, like the Grinnell brothers, had a long, productive life (1757–1837). He was born in White Marsh, Pennsylvania, studied law, and served as a brevet major in the Revolutionary War. Afterward he went into private practice, but soon government service called. In 1791 he was tapped to be a U.S. judge of the territory south of the River Ohio. When the territory became the state of Tennessee, he served as one of its first senators (1797–1815). Following that, Anderson became comptroller for the U.S. Treasury (1815–1816). He died a year after his retirement and is now interred in the Congressional Cemetery in Washington.

So, why was a street in a distant territory named for this public servant? The answer may be as buried as the exact location of his namesake street. Thus, we speculate. The purchase of Key West was, of course, an investment for Simonton and company. Did they name a piece of their real estate for a Treasury official in hope of ingratiating themselves? Their proposals for a Customs House, Marine Hospital, and other federally backed projects did, after all, receive approval and funding.

In any event, a military garrison was built in the location of one of the key's first streets. Complete with barracks for the enlisted men, officers' quarters, parade area, hospital, and small cemetery, it held its ground until the 1950s. In the meantime, neighboring Gulfside waters were dubbed Garrison Bight, a name suggesting the English origins of some Conch settlers. From the Middle English *bugun*, bight originally meant a bend or hollow. Eventually it also came to mean a curve or hollowing along a coastline, a bay.

The coastline so hollowed on Key West was called Pablo Beach (a.k.a. North Beach). Pablo Beach Road, an extension of Eaton Road wrapped around the Army barracks and hugged the shoreline. Long before it was paved and became Palm Drive, Pablo Beach Road provided a perfect venue for bicycle and horse races on the island.

Sam went over it all in his head as he looked at the charter boats moored in Garrison Bight. Here is where it had all begun. . . .

—Burt Hirschfeld, *Key West*

Peary Court

In the 1950s, when its wooden barracks were demolished, the Navy preserved the burial grounds and used the rest of the garrison for the same purpose as the Army had. In place of the barracks, the Navy constructed concrete-block bungalows and called them Peary Court. The development was short lived. In the 1970s the Key West Naval Station was closed and a lot of government property became surplus property. The bungalows at Peary Court were leveled, the land cleared and leased to the city for a dollar a year, and a recreational park created.

The Navy's retreat from the key was premature. By 1984 it was ready to return in force, and the park came under siege because the Navy wanted to reconstruct its housing development when the city's lease ran out in 1990. The softball field and other green spaces were in jeopardy. Preservationists and other aesthetes played hardball, but, despite their efforts and petitions (over five thousand people signed in protest), the Navy had its way. Today some one hundred sixty homes stand as testimony to the **Peary Court** resurrection.

Peary Court was named for onetime Key West resident Robert R. Peary. In 1881 the naval wharf in Key West was getting a makeover: iron pilings replaced wooden ones, and the pier was rebuilt with steel. Although Peary was in the Navy, he never was a line officer. It was as a civil engineer that he supervised the makeover. Years later Peary appropriated the title "Admiral" and went on to gain renown as an Arctic explorer. The pier was demolished by a hurricane in 1910, a year before Peary claimed to be the first person to reach the North Pole.

Robert Peary was a driven man. Born with a palate that turned his sibilant sounds into a self-conscious lisp, young Peary constantly strove toward self-improvement. By the time he was twenty-four years of age, he spoke slowly and carefully to conceal his impediment, and his quest for perfection was apparent: "I would like to acquire a name which could be an open sesame to circles of culture and refinement. I must have fame."

In 1886 he took a leave of absence from the Navy and began a quest that would dominate his next two decades and consume his life. He organized and led a number of expeditions that penetrated Arctic ice that had never been explored. The results varied and some discoveries proved to be erroneous, but by 1909 Peary was poised to make it to the top, to reach the North Pole—and he blew it.

At the age of fifty-three, after twenty-three years on the Arctic trail, Peary probably did accomplish the one thing he thought would set him apart from all others. Accompanied by five men, Peary claimed to have reached the Pole on April 6, 1909, but none of the five was a scientist who could verify his readings that they were indeed at the highest latitude. And most tragic of all was that this was no oversight: Peary believed that he alone had earned the right to be there, and he was not about to share his glory. But share it he would. Dr. Frederick Cook stole his thunder by claiming to have been at the Pole a year before Peary got there.

Peary's quest for fame and glory took its toll. Frostbite had taken the joints from all of his toes, and his detractors were at his heels. Dogged and obsessed by the controversy over whether he or Cook had been the first to reach the top, in 1920 Peary died a bitter man.

Jackson Square

. . . now it is the Methodists' nine o'clock turn to hold their service in the great hall of the county courthouse in Jackson Square, which all Key West denominations use, in round-robin hours for worship on Sundays.

—John Hersey, "God's Hint"

Jackson Square, platted between Whitehead and Thomas, Fleming and Southard, appears on William Whitehead's 1829 map of Key West. Two shaded rectangular drawings depict a courthouse and a jail within the 402-foot square. So, a courthouse may have been on the property before it was dedicated to the city solely for public use.

In 1876, years after he platted the land and drew the map, Whitehead indicated why the square is at its present site.

Writing from New Jersey, he said, "It was thought desirable that the public square should be located nearer the water, and the block between Fitzpatrick Street and Clinton Place was thought of." There was, however, already a building, probably a courthouse, used by county authorities on what is now Jackson Square, so practicality held sway and form followed function.

Besides providing a place of worship for Christians, the **Monroe County Courthouse** was also a place where couples were coupled for life, the dead mourned and remembered, children taught, and territorial and state court held. In 1889 the wooden courthouse was demolished to make way for a larger brick structure. As noted earlier, the **End of the Rainbow sign** marking one end of U.S. 1 sits beneath a majestic kapok tree within the square.

Jackson Square

The square was, of course, named for Andrew Jackson, United States commissioner and military governor of the Territory of East and West Florida. Soon after his appointment to be Florida's first governor, Jackson divided the territory into its first two counties: Escambia in the west and St. Johns along the eastern seaboard east of the Suwannee River. This, of course, was before much attention was paid to the nether end of the peninsula and its string of Keys.

Most of us are probably more familiar with Jackson as the enlarged visage that presides over the center of our multi-hued twenty-dollar bills. Jackson, often in error but never in doubt, was also our seventh president.

The courthouse in Key West was a stout and square brick building in a town of flimsy, leaning wooden homes, a monument to order and solidity in a place whose charm and wonder was the lack thereof.

—Laurence Shames, Tropical Depression

Clinton Place

Clinton Place is a vest-pocket park that is located at the junction of Greene, Whitehead, and Front (where it angled to wrap around the waterfront). Originally Clinton Place was a spacious triangular intersection. Like Jackson Square, it was dedicated for public use. In the late 1840s sponges torn from their sea beds and dried atop warehouse roofs were sold at auction in Clinton Place.

Today Clinton Place is still triangular, but it has shrunken to accommodate the traffic that cruises surrounding streets. Located in front of the 1891 U.S. Customs House, it now serves mainly as a commemorative site. In 1866 the Key West Navy Club erected a monument dedicated to the Union soldiers, sailors, and marines who died on the island during the War Between the States. Already garrisoned Gulfside at the army barracks, Union troops quickly occupied Ft. Taylor (and thus the city) at the onset of the war. The sentiment of many Key

Westers, however, may be indicated better by the wrought iron fence surrounding the granite monument than by the memorial itself. The fence was erected by Judge J.V. Harris, a Confederate veteran who left behind a plaque citing his deed.

Clinton Place is named after De Witt Clinton, a New York statesman and politician who served as mayor of New York City, governor of that state, and a U.S. senator. Besides establishing a tuition-free school system in New York, Clinton's most lasting accomplishment was his role in building the Erie Canal.

Governor Clinton planned the Erie Canal and oversaw the execution of those plans. The first important waterway dug in America, "Clinton's ditch" (so ridiculed by its naysayers) permitted goods to flow across the northern United States, from New York City to the far reaches of the Great Lakes. Its success precipitated development of towns along the canal and its Hudson River terminus, thus helping New York City attain its status as a great financial center.

A Confederate Veteran fences in a Union monument.

Mallory Square

The sun had begun to rise. In half a day, it would drop into the sea before a cheering throng at Mallory dock. Footloose, deracinated tourists, moving coordinates on a thousand chamber-of-commerce war maps . . .

     —Thomas McGuane, *Ninety-Two in the Shade*

Mallory Square, probably the best known of all Key West locales, is not a public square in the same sense as Jackson Square and Clinton Place. Named in the 1960s and fully developed by 1984, Mallory Square is, among other things, a bastion of pure capitalism. At sunset every day, throngs of tourists gather, ostensibly to watch the sun set, but more probably, one suspects, to be regaled by the evening spectacle.

  Bare-footed and bare-chested, an aesthetic Anglo fakir walks, sits, and lies down on broken glass, inviting some of the

Mallory Square.

lighter spectators to tread on him. A sturdier roustabout hefts motorcycles and washing machines aloft—and then balances them on his mouth! Cats jump through hoops of fire; a gasoline drinker exhales flames; a Caribbean islander, clad like our glass-crunching fakir but with definitely better body definition, performs acrobatic feats at these dockside Olympics. The cookie lady pedals her wares astride a three-wheeler. A holdout from the Sixties performs oldies-but-goodies. And, of course, the hat is passed after every performance, the guitar case ever open for contributions. T-shirt stalls, sea shell shops, hair braiding and beading, corn rowing, and every manner of kitsch is to be found on the square. Some observers have compared this nightly extravaganza to the medieval tradition of strolling minstrels and wandering troubadours. Possibly, but to others might not it all simply appear to be America on the make in an open-air mall?

Its 1984 makeover came complete with pointed rather than rounded pillars, the better to keep those pesky pelicans and other aquatic birds from squatting on them and fouling the venue. Cruise ships use the refurbished square as a day base from which their passengers can disembark and see Key West.

Today's Mallory Square has its roots embedded in the sea muck beneath its smooth surface. Over a hundred years before it became entertainment-central-at-sunset, this harbor area was home to a half dozen wharves, their warehouses, and a number of chandlers. Besides serving as a supply point for a dependent island, the area was also the locus of the wrecking business. Cargoes salvaged were unloaded here, stored, and eventually sold at auction. Then, in 1873, after the decline of wrecking, the precursor of today's luxury cruise ships was launched.

Clyde Mallory started the Mallory Steamship Company, a shipping firm that served New York City, Key West, and Galveston, Texas. For decades, the Mallory and Company ships tied up at Mallory Docks when in home port. By 1912 the company had become part of the Atlantic, Gulf, and West Indies Steamship Lines. In the 1960s, the docks were upgraded and named for another Mallory, Stephen R.

Stephen's mother, Ellen Russell Mallory, was one of the first settlers on the island. Born at Carrick-on-Suir, Ireland, in 1792, Miss Russell immigrated to Trinidad to live with her uncle when she was thirteen years old. By sixteen she had married Charles John Mallory, a Connecticut construction engineer. In 1820 the family moved to the United States, eventually settling in Key West in 1823. In poor health, John quickly learned that the subtropics were no panacea. Soon after their arrival, he and their eldest son died.

Mrs. Mallory stayed on and raised their other son. Until her death in 1855, she ran the only comfortable boarding house on the island. As indicated by a historical marker that stands in Clinton Place, it was called **Coconut Grove House** and stood **near Greene and Front Streets**. It was used as a residence by her son and grandson after her death and, in light of their prominence, became the key's center of social and intellectual life. Built in 1839, Coconut Grove House stood for over fifty years. Purchased by the Navy during its 1890 expansion, the sturdy, but elegant, two-story home was leveled to make way for the Navy base that has become Truman Annex.

Besides earning her livelihood as an innkeeper, Mrs. Mallory served Key Westers as a volunteer nurse. She was best remembered for the courage she displayed in treating the island's victims of yellow fever, a disease believed at the time to be contagious.

Her surviving son, Stephen R. Mallory, was born in Trinidad in 1812 and immigrated to Key West with the family. He was educated at boarding schools in Mobile, Alabama, and Nazareth, Pennsylvania. Upon returning home, he was soon (1833) appointed by President Jackson to be the U.S. customs inspector. Later in the 1830s, Mallory read law for the bar, to which he was admitted in 1840. While practicing privately and becoming an authority on maritime and wrecker's law, Mallory also served as city marshal and collector of the customs.

Among his more lasting civic contributions was his role in relocating the lighthouse to its present location farther inland. (The 1846 hurricane had destroyed the coastal lighthouse at Whitehead's Point.) It is, however, as a U.S. senator that Mallory is most renowned. Elected in 1851, Senator Mallory capitalized on his maritime expertise and soon became chairman of the Senate Naval Committee. In this capacity he was one of the first to advocate the extension of the railroad to Key West. Mallory believed that, from a strategic perspective, the United States would benefit from having a gateway into the Caribbean and southern Gulf of Mexico. Similarly, in 1856 he pushed for a stronger naval presence on the strategically located island.

Ironically, his advocacy would come back to haunt him. Though not a staunch secessionist, Mallory heeded the wishes of his constituents and withdrew from the Senate when Florida seceded from the Union in January 1861. By the outbreak of war in April 1861, he had been appointed secretary of the Confederate Navy. His most memorable contribution to the war effort was authorizing work on what became the world's first successful ironclad vessel. The U.S.S. *Merrimac* was converted into the C.S.S. *Virginia,* and then proceeded to destroy a good portion of the Union fleet. On land, however, the rebels were not faring as well. When Norfolk, Virginia, was evacuated, the *Virginia* became a ship without a homeport. Too draught-heavy to join the evacuation up the James River, she was scuttled and burned by her crew.

After the War Between the States, Mallory lived in Lagrange Troop County, Georgia, for a while, and then moved to Pensacola in 1866. There he practiced law until his death on November 9, 1873. He is buried in St. Michael's Cemetery in Pensacola.

Mallory Square

The Civil War came and they built two blockade runners for the rebellion . . . while Stephen Mallory left town to become Secretary of the Confederate Navy.
> —Thomas McGuane, *Panama*

In recent years, Mallory Square has broadened its scope and included attractions of historic interest. The **Mallory Museum** at Hospitality House now occupies a corner of the square, and the **Key West–Florida Keys Historical Military Memorial** graces the back of the square. The memorial has inherited the forward ten-inch gun turret that was salvaged from the U.S.S. *Maine*. It is displayed near a set of nine interpretive plaques that tell the role the military has played in providing security for the Keys, Florida, and the nation since the Anti-piracy Campaign of the 1820s.

Lanes and Alleys

"I live on a lane called love. Love Lane's behind the library. Key West is filled with funny little lanes with cute names."
— Thomas Sanchez, *Mile Zero*

Wall Street

K ey West, like New York, has its Wall Street—and both are rooted in wealth. Key West's is named for William H. Wall, a dignified Englishman who, according to Browne in *Key West: The Old and the New*, spoke with "the perfect diction of the cultured men of that nation."

Shipwrecked off the coast of Key West in 1830, Wall must have believed in providence: he stayed and a year later established the island's first cigar factory. Wall located his factory on Front Street, between Duval and Fitzpatrick. His fifty employees rolled the best leaf from Havana before a fire sent it all up in smoke in 1859. Wall made his fortunes as a merchant and entrepreneur, although his attempt to manufacture salt failed. He was also a civic leader, a member of the town council, an inaugural member of St. Paul's Episcopal Church, and the first state senator from Monroe County.

Wall Street was originally called Water Street. After the development of wharves and warehouses along the waterfront, the land was gradually built up out to the deep channel of the harbor. Water Street began as a path that meandered along the front between Front Street and the harbor, from Whitehead to Simonton. Unlike Jacksonville, which renamed one of its Water Streets by spelling it backward, Retaw, in 1847 Key West honored a leading citizen with its name change.

Today, Wall Street can hardly be classified as a street: it merely borders Mallory Square to Duval Street. Here, however, is still a reminder of the activity that once dominated this area. Key West's first fireproof warehouse, a Wall and Company structure, still stands on his namesake "street." It is now home to **Cayo Hueso y Habana**, a restaurant and historeum that celebrates island and Cuban culture through its food and history.

Wolkowsky Lane

We drove in silence down Duval to the Pier House where she was staying. She got out and flounced to the motel door without a backward glance. Oh well.

—Jim Harrison, A Good Day to Die

Wolkowsky Lane is named for Key West entrepreneur David W. Wolkowsky. The Wolkowskys have been in Key West for generations. In 1912, when the railroad arrived, David's grandfather was running his Island City Supply House. But neither granddad nor dad affected the island as has David, who is best known for his creation of the **Pier House**.

In 1963 Wolkowsky bought the Gulf Oil waterfront property between Duval and Simonton for less than a shotgun handyman special goes for today. He then relocated the nineteenth-century Porter Steamship office from the old Key West–Havana ferry dock out into the harbor. Starting off with a restaurant, he gradually built today's Pier House complex around the relocated office.

Tift's Alley

Mr. Tift says to his wife that these Negroes are property. . . . Mrs. Tift says to her husband that he is mistaken. These are not chattels but "human souls, just like you and me, my dear Asa."

—John Hersey, "Just Like You and Me"

Nearby, running a short distance between Wall and Front, is Tift's Alley. This is another of Key West's locales named for an individual more deserving of an in-depth biography than the cursory treatment that follows.

Asa Tift was originally from Mystic, Connecticut. By 1836 he and brother Amos had moved to Key West and, as owners of a dry goods store, were firmly established on the island. Asa, however, made a considerable fortune not in merchandising but in shipping. In conjunction with his enterprises, he built one of the first wharves to dot the waterfront. (In 1838, just before William Whitehead departed, he drew a sketch of the island from its cupola.)

Tift's Alley was created in 1837 as a right-of-way to Tift's wharf and dock property. Eventually his interests expanded so that he needed all of present-day Mallory Square to contain them. One enterprise was the sale of natural ice. Before 1890 ice had to be imported. Ice shipped down from Maine was stored in a thick-walled warehouse that was built in 1841 and still stands at **402 Wall Street**. Nowadays it is home to the **Shell Warehouse**. Adjacent to the icehouse was a regular warehouse. Today it houses the **Greater Key West Chamber of Commerce Visitor's Center**.

In addition to his shipping and other interests, Tift was a major landholder and forester. Tifton, a town he founded in South Georgia, bears his surname. Heart-of-white-pine lumber from his holdings was shipped to Key West, where it was used in the construction of his home, a Spanish Colonial mansion located at **907 Whitehead**. It was completed in 1851. Eighty years later a young American couple who had been living in France purchased it.

Tift was a staunch secessionist and segregationist. In early 1861 he represented Key West at the Constitutional Convention that ratified Florida's secession from the Union. In

May of that year, at the onset of Civil War hostilities, Tift left Yankee-occupied Key West.

Wolfson Lane

Wolfson Lane is another of the island's byways named for a modern entrepreneur. Formerly known as Exchange Street, on December 20, 1970, its name was changed to honor Mitchell Wolfson and his family. Wolfson, a successful businessman, made a philanthropic move that sparked a movement.

In 1960 he purchased the **Geiger House**, home of wrecker John Geiger and generations of his family, and converted it into the **Audubon House**. Though John James Audubon, the naturalist and ornithologist, never stayed there (it was built after his 1832 visit), the house and garden at **205 Whitehead** stand as a monument to his work. Inspired by Wolfson, the newly founded Old Island Restoration Committee became more active and productive in its community restoration and preservation efforts.

A wee little lane, Wolfson, like Tift, sprints between Front and Wall and borders the **Key West Memorial Sculpture Garden**.

Nearby, between Greene and Caroline, is **Telegraph Alley**. It derived its name from the location of the International Ocean Telegraph Company and later the Western Union Telegraph Office at its corner with Greene, where the Emerald Lady jewelry store stands today.

Right-angling off Telegraph Alley and running a hundred feet or so up to Duval is another of Key West's "streets" barely deserving of the distinction. **Charles Street** is named for

Charles Tift, one of the island's early mapmakers.

A block over and toward the harbor, **Weaver Alley** runs off Simonton between Greene and Fort Streets. George E. Weaver, a grocer and chandler, was another early settler and inaugural member of St. Paul's. After Key West became an incorporated city in 1832, G.E. Weaver won election as one of its six councilmen. In 1838, no longer a councilman, Weaver and others vigorously protested the enforcement of an ordinance that levied an occupational tax on businesses. As you may recall, the furor that grew out of this matter led to the resignation of Mayor Whitehead and his departure from Key West.

Dey Street and More

On his first morning back in Key West Tommy picked up Daryl and headed for Dey Street.

—Stuart Woods, *Choke*

A block away, also running off Simonton, is Dey Street. With Dey, we reestablish the New Jersey–Key West connection. William Whitehead Sr., father of John, William, and siblings whose names we have seen on the streets of Old Town, lived on Dey Street in Newark.

Farther inland, off Elizabeth, is a pair of lanes hardly a dozen paces from each other. **Higgs Lane** is named for the Reverend Gilbert Higgs, pastor of St. Paul's for a record thirteen years (1890–1903). A native of St. George, Bermuda, Higgs was an avid gardener who created an ornamental garden, the pride of the island, on church grounds. Higgs died in Atlanta in 1911, but his ties to his adopted home were so strong that his remains were returned for services and burial in the City Cemetery.

Donkey Milk Lane is the twin closer to Eaton and so named for its proximity to **Donkey Milk House** on that larger thoroughfare. During the Depression, when times were especially tough in Key West, the owner of the house at **611 Eaton** kept a drove of donkeys in a stable to the rear. Every morning those too poor to afford cow's milk were welcome to take the milk provided by the mares. Access to the stable was via Elizabeth, down the narrow alley that runs behind the houses facing Eaton.

A half block away, between Eaton and Caroline, is **Peacon Lane**, once known as Grunt Bone Alley. Grunts and grits were long-time staples on the island. Presumably, this alley became a dumping ground for the remains of a species of fish named for its ability to make grunting sounds. The alley was renamed for Richard Peacon, Key West's most prominent grocer. Henry Faulkner, eccentric, artist, and fast friend of Tennessee Williams, lived at **328 Peacon Lane**—with his live-in goat Alice!

. . . Julie came back around the block, down Peacon Lane, past swing chairs on porches, railings and cacti, stubby driveways and trash cans.

—Tom Corcoran, *Bone Island Mambo*

Sawyer Lane, right-angling off William Street, meets Roberts Lane, which comes off Caroline. There are a couple of Sawyers resting nearby who could lay claim to the lane. James (1797–1829) and Captain John H. Sawyer (1802–1843) are the oldest residents of City Cemetery. Their remains were exhumed from a settlement graveyard and reburied in a fresh plot in 1847. "General" Abe Sawyer, Key West's most famous dwarf, is also in the cemetery. Born in 1862, he traveled with various performing groups and circuses throughout his career. Always aspiring to greater stature, the "General" got his wish at death: he is buried in a full-sized grave. Sawyer Lane, alas, is not named for someone as colorful as the "General" or as historic as the Sawyer brothers were. It is named for Benjamin Sawyer, who was mayor of Key West from 1844 to 1846.

As for **Roberts Lane**, my search for the "real" Roberts is still inconclusive, but there are a number of possibilities to choose from. According to Browne, there is the "colored" Roberts, a friend of secessionist Stephen Mallory, who joined the future Confederate secretary of the Navy when, as young men, they went serenading the island's belles. A daughter of master wrecker Captain Francis B. Watlington married Joseph P. Roberts, a well-known merchant. Following its destruction in 1909, the **Sparks Chapel (729 Fleming Street)** was rebuilt by Reverend W. H. F. Roberts. And we have James A. Roberts, a man of color who served as sheriff during Reconstruction. But again, the nod will probably go to yet another politician, E. Monroe Roberts, who served as a county commissioner in the early 1900s.

Nearby, but coming off Eaton, is **Gecko Lane**, recently named so the postman would know where to deliver the mail.

No doubt you'll know when you are near. Just listen, as did the Malays (from whose language *gekoq* came), for the distinctive sound of these wall lizards.

Thompson Lane, between Grinnell and Frances, appears to have been named for the Thompson family. Nordberg Thomsen, a Norwegian who was shipwrecked near Key West, must have liked what he saw when he came ashore. Altering his first name (which means North Mountain) and anglicizing his surname to *Thompson*, he remained in Key West and sired a large family that helped him run his diverse enterprises. There was fishing and fish-processing, marine hardware and tackle, cigar-box manufacturing, guava jelly production, trucking and turtle-soup canning, the operation of Thompson docks, and more. Norberg's grandson, Charles, and his wife, Lorine, became good friends of Pauline and Ernest Hemingway. Norberg Thompson, Charles's older brother, was elected mayor in 1915, served on various city and county commissions, and was active on the Overseas Highway Committee and Everglades National Park Commission.

Stickney has the distinction of designating two lanes in Key West: one in our present area, near Peary Court, and the other off South Roosevelt near the airport. Apparently named for Joseph Stickney, they honor a man who joined a hundred other Key Westers in pledging allegiance to the Union at the beginning of the Civil War. On May 16, 1861, Stickney et al. formed a volunteer company dedicated to preserving the honor of the American flag and quelling the rebellion.

The man for whom **Curry Lane** is designated is far from obscure. William Curry was born on Green Turtle Key in the Bahamas and migrated to Key West when he was sixteen years old. He immediately went into business with Weaver and

Baldwin, switched over to Wall and Company when they closed shop, and was on his own before his twenty-third birthday. Over the next fifty years, he amassed a fortune through hard work and shrewd investment. Owner of the island's largest ship chandlery, Curry was also a banker, merchant, and owner of wrecking schooners and the clipper ship *Stephen R. Mallory*. Reputedly the richest man in Florida, he died in 1896. A train of more than seventy carriages bore his remains to the cemetery, where a toppled urn symbolizing death at a ripe old age marks his grave site.

. . . Arty looked around and wondered for the thousandth time why he'd stayed so long in the rented four-room transient-looking cottage on Nassau Lane.

—Laurence Shames, *Sunburn*

Running parallel to Curry is **Stump Lane**, once called Garrison due to its location near the Army barracks. Stump Lane is named for the Charles Stump family. Nassau Lane, of obvious origin, is nearby. Its backyard neighbor, Lowe Lane, is accessible from Grinnell. Though named for Charles W. Lowe (City Council, 1911), the more renowned Lowe is Caroline (1833–1924). A Confederate sympathizer during the War Between the States, she continually violated town law by waving the Rebel flag from atop her home. Union troops would dutifully search her premises for the incriminating evidence, but they never found the well-hidden Stars and Bars.

On the other side of Grinnell, Lowe turns into **Cornish Lane**. Like the **AME Chapel** on at **704 Whitehead**, this lane is named in honor of Andrew "Sandy" Cornish. Born a slave in the 1790s, in 1839, with the help of his wife Lillah, he bought his freedom. Years later a fire destroyed the documents conferring his freed status, and he was captured by slave hunters intent on selling him at market in New Orleans. Sandy escaped and mutilated himself to assure that his market value would be diminished. In the late 1840s, he and Lillah moved to Key West, where they maintained the best fruit and vegetable farm on the key. In 1865 Cornish helped establish the African Methodist Episcopal (AME) Church, where he preached.

Hibiscus Lane, about eighty feet past Cornish toward the harbor, also runs off Grinnell. Hibiscus was formerly known as

Billy Goat Lane. Closer yet to the Gulf is **Fletcher's Lane**. It may have been named after Silas Fletcher, whose management of the Appleby-Snyder store on Indian Key led to permanent settlement of the island.

Cornish Chapel, 704 Whitehead. Sandy Cornish preached here.

Lanes and Alleys

The police pulled the big cruiser up alongside of me and kept it at walking speed until I nipped up Lopez Lane and bought an aloe plant for a dime.

—Thomas McGuane, *Panama*

Lopez Lane once provided the solitude that fueled writer Philip Caputo's work. There, near the end of the cul-de-sac, in a cigar-maker's cottage that he converted into a studio, Caputo wrote *Delcorso's Gallery*, a novel depicting the obscenity of war-torn Beirut. Caputo's hideaway was located on a strip named for a martyr of another conflict. "General" Narciso Lopez, a former colonel in the Spanish Royal Army, was a Cuban revolutionary who fled to Key West in 1849. After hearing his tales of Cuba's oppression under Spanish rule, many rallied to the cause. In 1850 Lopez and some five hundred followers invaded Cuba, inflicted casualties, and escaped back to Key West. A year later he was less fortunate: he landed a smaller expedition at Bahia Honda, but failed to rally many Cubans to his side. He was captured and executed in September 1851.

"Cuba libre!" the rallying cry Lopez fervidly taught them, soon became . . . the nickname of a certain kind of rum drink with which . . . they lubricated their bravado.

—John Hersey, "Cuba Libre"

Calabash Alley, within the same block as Lopez but jutting off Fleming, is named for the tropical calabash gourd, vine, and evergreen tree. Once devoid of its fruit and dried out, the hard-shelled gourd has a variety of uses. Natives of the tropics have used it as a drinking vessel and cooking pot, and it can be fashioned into a smoking pipe of the type favored by Sherlock Holmes.

The first Conch Train of the day rumbled past, its driver explaining that the sapodilla tree . . . was the source of chicle used to make chewing gum. He drove on, ignoring the rare bottle-gourd tree, the calabash, across the street.

—Tom Corcoran, *Bone Island Mambo*

Pinder is a familiar name in Key West. Sylvanus Pinder, a gregarious fellow who had a large following, took his turn as one of the island's "Kings of the Wreckers." A number of Pinders were active in the Methodist Church, and William M. Pinder, for whom **Pinder Lane** is probably named, was a city council-man in 1911.

Love can generate some confusion—and **Love Lane** is no exception. Some maps show two Loves, one coming off Fleming and another off Southard, but not meeting mid-block. Other maps indicate that Gwynn Street, named for former mayor and cigar tycoon E. O. Gwynn, is the lane that runs off Southard. And yet another source cites Johnny Cake Lane as making up the northern half of Love Lane. At one time, perhaps it did. But if you're looking for flat cornmeal cakes baked on a griddle (*jonikin*, of Amerindian origin), you'd better go elsewhere. As confirmed by the loving couple who resides on the Fleming Street side of the lane, both are now called Love Lane. It seems that they don't meet because the bungalow that bisects the lane was built on the sly and, over the decades, has been grandfathered in and let stand.

Russell Lane could have been named after a number of prominent Key Westers. There is Circuit Court Clerk Eugene W. Russell (early 1900s); William A. Russell, proprietor of the Russell House Hotel; and the Honorable Albert J. Russell, state superintendent of public instruction. One would like to believe, however, that it was named for "Sloppy Joe" Russell, who led a full life but, according to his gravestone, died an early death.

JOSEPH P. RUSSELL
DEC. 8, 1888
JUNE 20, 1941
THO LOST TO SIGHT,
TO MEMORY DEAR

Artic Court is another unsolved mystery. Did a mapmaker think she was being humorous in dubbing a spot in the subtropics for a polar region, only to find that she was orthographically challenged? Or was someone merely following through on the Peary/Grinnell connections to Key West? Whatever the case, to get back on terra firma we needn't go far: we already know that neighboring Free School Alley once led to the island's first public school.

Now back in town, we see that **Bahama Street**, once known as Chicken Bone Alley, serves primarily as a parking lot for **Fausto's Food Palace** today. In the past a small cigar factory and a Chinese hand laundry had been located along this byway.

Appelrouth Lane, between Duval and Whitehead near Southard, is also downtown. Rechristened in 1981 for Jewish merchant William H. "Billy" Appelrouth, it had been known as **Smith Lane** (L. Windsor Smith) for decades.

Finally, **Babcock Lane**, midway between Duval and Whitehead off Fleming, is named after George L. Babcock, Key West mayor at the turn of the century and a leader of the island's ill-fated temperance movement. Salud!

Porter Lane

Soon after Florida became an American territory, President Monroe realized the strategic importance of Key West and took measures to turn it into the Gibraltar of the Gulf. His secretary of the Navy, the Honorable Smith Thompson, dispatched young Lieutenant Matthew C. Perry to secure the island.

Perry was also ordered to survey the island and its harbor, and officially declare it a part of Florida. He arrived on March 25, 1822, and promptly hoisted the Stars and Stripes above an island he would soon rename. In honor of his boss, he called it Thompson's Island; in homage to Commodore Rogers, president of the Naval Board, he dubbed the harbor Port Rogers. Perry, of course, went on to become a commodore himself. Decades later he sailed into Tokyo Bay and negotiated a trade treaty, thereby "opening" Japan to the West.

Commander James Biddle succeeded Perry on Thompson's Island, but the powers-that-be were not pleased with his efforts in fighting piracy. Soon he was replaced by Commodore David Porter. As the commander of the West Indian Squadron, a fleet of seventeen ships and over a thousand sailors, Porter was charged with ridding the region of those pesky pirates and overzealous wreckers. With the aid of a number of shallow-draft vessels and barges, Porter flushed the buccaneers from their havens throughout the Keys. But he didn't stop with the Keys: he pursued them throughout the Caribbean, well into Spanish territory, and was rewarded for his zeal with a court martial that charged him with exceeding his orders.

Porter's tenure at base port was equally as tumultuous. He began his reign by attempting to rename the island Allenton (in honor of one of his officers, Lieutenant William H. Allen, who was killed in a skirmish with pirates off the coast of Cuba) and by attempting to turn it into a citadel. Porter's justification was his contention that the island was U.S. government property because Simonton's claim of proprietorship was still being determined by a congressional commission. Copying the Parisian plan, he proposed a starlike pattern of streets that would radiate out from central plazas.

In the event of civil disturbance, artillery could then be deployed from the plazas straight down the streets. This plan, of course, never materialized and, thanks to first surveyor H. L. Barnum and subsequent mapmaker William Whitehead, Key West ended up with today's grid pattern. But Porter did build five military roads, one of which, along with a Porter Place, he named for himself. (It later became Main Street; soon after that, it was given its current name, Whitehead.)

The Porter Lane we find in the Truman Annex, near Emma Street, was not named for the commodore. That honor was reserved for Dr. Joseph Y. Porter, Florida's first public health officer.

Born at home (**429 Caroline Street**) on October 21, 1847, baby Joseph never knew his dad, who died six weeks after his birth. His mother died twelve years later, so Joseph was raised by his maternal grandmother. During the Civil War the family moved to New York. Joseph was educated in New Jersey and went to Philadelphia's Jefferson Medical College to become a physician. During this time he kept the home fires burning, returned, and married Louisa Curry, eldest daughter of William and Euphemia Curry.

By now an assistant surgeon in the Army, Lieutenant Porter served a hitch in the Dry Tortugas, at Ft. Jefferson, followed by service in Laredo, Texas, and other Army posts in the Southwest. Discharged due to a heart condition, Dr. Porter returned home and went into private practice. It was in Jacksonville, however, that he really distinguished himself. While he was visiting there, a yellow fever epidemic broke out. Pressed into service, "Big Joe" Porter took command of the emergency and directed treatment for the 5,000 victims who had contracted the disease. Only four hundred died. Doctor Porter received a gold watch, keys to the city, and due recognition.

When the legislature, in special session, established a State Board of Health in 1889, he was appointed its executive secretary and state public health officer. He served until his retirement in 1917. Dr. Porter remained active until 1927, when he died in the same room in which he was born eighty years earlier.

Little Streets

We strolled past La Lechoneria toward the synagogue. He knew all the little streets and stared up and down with sad affection.

—Thomas McGuane, *Panama*

 ere we'll start again on one side of the island and make our way across town to Eisenhower Drive, near Garrison Bight, on the other side.

DeKalb Street, Covington Avenue, and Fort Street

. . . I watched money change hands on the corner of Emma, saw the dead end at Fort Street, the old Navy building, the green eight-foot chain-link fence with barbed wire up top.

—Tom Corcoran, *Octopus Alibi*

This set of "little streets" is near Ft. Zachary Taylor, hence the obvious naming of Fort Street. Covington Avenue is a different

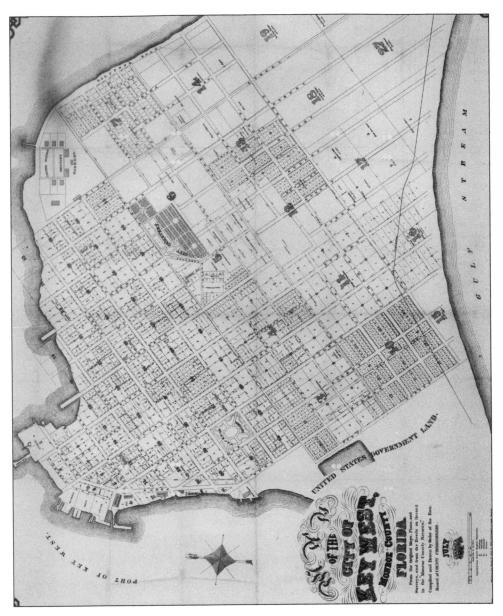

*By 1874 development had spread to United Street,
three blocks past today's Truman Avenue.*

matter: we only know that it was named for a military man somehow connected to the artillery batteries at the fort. DeKalb, on the other hand, is a name that warrants entry in every American encyclopedia and history book.

"Baron" Johann DeKalb was born in Bavaria, Germany, in 1721. At birth, however, he did not inherit his title. This he would add later, presumably to bolster his credentials, for De Kalb was a soldier of fortune of the highest order. Signing on with the French in 1743, he rose through the ranks to become a French brigadier general. In 1877 he joined the Marquis de Lafayette when the French nobleman went abroad to aid American revolutionaries. Appointed a major general by the Continental Congress, DeKalb was at Valley Forge with General Washington and later served as second-in-command to General Horatio Gates in the Carolinas. There, when Gates suffered a major defeat in Camden, DeKalb met his waterloo. Decades later Lafayette commemorated DeKalb's service to the Revolution by laying the cornerstone of the Camden monument that honors our fallen hero.

So, why is the street named after DeKalb? Why not a Gate's Way or Lafayette Lane? Could the Carolina–Key West connection explain this? We know that a number of Conchs are descended from Carolina Tories who fled to the Bahamas. Also, other Carolinians more faithful to a republic that DeKalb died fighting for have migrated directly to Key West.

Little Streets

Angela, Petronia, and Olivia Streets

Shaw jogged back to the car and drove over to the house on Olivia Street. It was a white shotgun house built almost a hundred years earlier by a rich Cuban cigar maker.

—James W. Hall, *Bones of Coral*

This trio of ladies make their way from Fort all the way to Garrison Bight. **Olivia**, the only street that goes through uninterrupted, is named for Olivia Curry Wall, daughter of William H. and Petronia Wall, whom we met off Mallory Square. Midway on her trip cross-island, Olivia skirts the City Cemetery. Across from the cemetery, running along the 800 block, is a row of shotgun cottages built to house some of the key's blue-collar workers. Once home to fishermen, cigar rollers, and sponge harvesters, these structures now only echo the island's ups and downs.

Another health food shop on Olivia.

Graham and Louise Wells lived in a large house on Petronia Street,
not far from the old naval base, now closed down. . . .

—Burt Hirschfeld, *Key West*

Olivia's mom must have kept close tabs on her. A block
over and running parallel is **Petronia**, named for Petronia
Martinelli Wall, wife of William and mother of Olivia. By all
accounts she was quite a catch in her day. A beauty of either
Spanish or Minorcan descent who came on island in the early
settlement days, she was regarded as the reigning belle of her
time. Petronia Street, broken by a tangle of lanes near the
cemetery, continues on the other side through to Eisenhower
Drive.

City Hall squatted on Angela Street where it crossed Simonton, wide
steps leading up to the double glass doors. . . . A buff-colored two
story structure, it possessed little architectural interest, a design
intended to camouflage the stuffy mediocrity which infects municipal
governments everywhere.

—Burt Hirschfeld, *Key West*

Angela Street, also broken in a few places, is probably
named for Angela S. Mallory, wife of Stephen R. Originally the
division line (outer boundary) of town, the path was unnamed
for years. Now it borders City Cemetery—where Angela can
look upon the gravestones of two of her children, Ellen

Josephine ("aged 3 years 7 mos.") and Francis Moreno M. ("aged 2 years 4 mos."), buried alongside grandmother Ellen in the family plot.

As just indicated by Hirschfeld, Angela Street is home to City Hall, now named in honor of Josephine Parker, who served as city clerk for years. Parker, who suffered a stroke at a city council meeting, died in the late 1990s. The lane that runs next to City Hall, behind the inn that was once the Tilton Hilton, and in front what used to be the Greyhound Bus Station is also named for this dedicated civil servant.

As we move away from City Hall, we come across a couple of visual delights that better define Angela Street: one of elegant, antiquated lines; the other shrouded in funky mystery. The **Burton House** is of historic and histrionic note. Built in the last century from lumber shipped down the Mississippi, this Queen Anne cottage was purchased by Shakespearean scholar,

Burton House. Liz probably slept here.

115

actor, and director Philip Burton in 1974. Years before moving to Key West, Philip had trained actor Richard Burton in his craft. Reportedly, Richard's wife, Elizabeth Taylor, visited often before Philip died in 1995. Located at **608 and the corner of Whitmarsh Lane**, the Burton House presides atop the summit of Solares Hill.

At the **corner of Angela and Margaret**, across from the cemetery, sits another cottage whose owner has imbued it with histrionics of a funkier nature. Framed of natural, weathered wood, it hunkers down behind the unlikeliest of walls. There, suspended from re-bar, concrete seems to drip to the ground, forming a hedge that reflects back at you from small round mirrors embedded within.

Re-bar and dripping concrete form a Key West landmark across from the cemetery.

Little Streets

Right on Angela where all the bottles are set in dripping concrete, Catherine spotted a young man in a shiny suit.

—Thomas McGuane, *Panama*

Williams Alley

Williams Alley is located in what was called Jungle Town in less racially sensitive times. I had often wondered why so many African Americans bear the surname Williams. The answer is so obvious that I had overlooked it. Williams is also a very common Anglo name. Upon emancipation, freed slaves either took on the names of their former masters or randomly selected ones from the population at large. Discovering why this particular byway is so named has been more difficult.

We do have Crazy Jim Williams, whose insanity was induced when, as a youngster, he witnessed the massacre on Indian Key. For years he wandered the streets of Key West crying, "The Indians are coming." And we have a William H. Williams, who dealt with labor unrest among the island's Cuban cigar makers in the 1890s. Given its location, though, perhaps this alley is named for Jesse and William Williams, a couple of African Americans who emigrated from St. Augustine.

Hutchinson Lane, Shavers Lane, et al.

A block over is **Hutchinson Lane**. In 1892, a W. H. Hutchinson began publishing a newspaper called the *Gulf*

Pennant, a name suggested by the Honorable Colonel W. D. Chipley (a railroad official for whom Chipley in north Florida was renamed). The paper folded on Independence Day, 1893.

Shavers Lane, between Whitehead and Duval, is named for a black resident of the area. Nearby, off Duval, we have **Whalton Lane**, of which more is known of its progenitor.

Joseph C. Whalton was one of the first Anglo settlers, arriving on Key West even before Simonton bought the island from Salas. There he met another recent immigrant, a young woman of Spanish descent. They married and raised a family whose descendants are still in Key West.

A teetotaler, in 1848 Joseph helped Francis Watlington organize "Sons of Temperance," a sobriety society that survived until Civil War times. No doubt, Whalton would have been nonplussed to learn that a present-day descendant, Michael Whalton, not only became manager of Sloppy Joe's but also organized the Hemingway Days Festival, an event celebrating anything but sobriety.

Also between Whitehead and Duval, a couple of blocks toward the harbor, is **Aronovitz Lane**. Abe Aronovitz, like his contemporary, "Billy" Appelrouth, was a Jewish merchant. Both are buried in the sector of the City Cemetery marked "B'nai Zion."

Mickens Lane is near Aronovitz. Formerly called Guava Lane, it is now named for the Mickens family. And across Duval, at the paw of Center Street (once known as Cat Alley), is **DuPont Lane**. Charles DuPont was the second of Key West's black sheriffs. He served from 1889 to 1893.

Pierce Lane, off Simonton, puts us back in uncharted territory. Was it named after Charles R. Pierce, stalwart member of the community who sat on the Board of Public Works and Board of Directors of the Island City National Bank, the same Pierce who helped establish the Hargrove Institute at the turn of the century? Or was the lane named for "Young" Lewy Pierce, a local lad fast with his fists, but destined to end up a "sedate capitalist" retired in the Miami area? Then again, perhaps the honor goes to Louis W. Pierce. In 1885 Louis was granted a franchise to operate street car lines anywhere passable outside corporate limits.

Whitmarsh Lane, a couple of blocks over and next to the Burton House at the summit of Solares Hill, is named for the Whitmarsh family, a member of which played a small role in the island's folklore. On April 28, 1931, Mary F. Whitmarsh was witness to the transfer of the property at 907 Whitehead Street to one Ernest Miller Hemingway.

Baker's Lane, Galveston Lane, Poorhouse Lane, Windsor Lane, and Passover Street

Peachy lived alone in a small house he owned on Baker's Lane, three blocks from Patrick and Lee's.

—John Leslie, *Killer in Paradise*

Baker's Lane is an L-shaped cul-de-sac off Elizabeth, near its intersection with Angela. Named for Benjamin P. Baker, contractor, lumber-yard owner, and undertaker, this lane's most prominent feature is the house on the corner of Elizabeth that Benjamin built as a wedding gift to his daughter in 1885. His workers, finally freed from the tedium of banging coffins together, went all out in every manner of gingerbread ornamenta-

A peace that eluded him.

tion—and built a structure that resembles a wedding cake!

Down the lane, at **709**, is another place of distinction. Formerly it was the residence of writer James Leo Herlihy, author of *Midnight Cowboy*. This cottage stands out because of its large, triangular stained-glass window beneath the apex and, at ground level, the balusters that Herlihy had cut into peace symbols, a peace that apparently eluded him, for he committed suicide.

There was a writer on Elizabeth Street who had some success and broke down or burned out.

—Thomas McGuane, *Panama*

. . . all newcomers aren't bad. Some of them bailed people out. . . . Jamie Herlihy, the guy who wrote Midnight Cowboy, *was always doing that.*

—Tom Corcoran, *Octopus Alibi*

Over on the other side of Solares Hill are a couple of entries that are self-explanatory. **Galveston Lane** is named for the Texan coastal city that was served by the Mallory Steamship Company, and off Windsor, on **Poorhouse Lane**, a poorhouse was once tucked away.

Therefore, on Galveston Lane, I made arrangements to purchase a parrot who said Jesus, Mary, Joseph at the trilling of a bell, the sight of a monstrance or a cracker.

—Thomas McGuane, *Panama*

Windsor Lane functions more like a street than a lane. It angles off Elizabeth, intersects Passover at the cemetery, and proceeds for blocks, well past Truman Avenue. L. Windsor Smith was Key West's first prominent attorney. In the 1840s he served twice as district attorney. He must have also been a bit of a land speculator. In 1847 he bought thirty-five acres of land bordering Old Town and promptly sold a portion of it to the

Dedicated to a writer fond of anagrams.

city, where the first one hundred plots of its new cemetery were marked off.

Writer John Hersey, who died in 1993, spent many a winter working in a compound on Windsor, near its intersection with Passover. Friends of Libraries USA has mounted a poignant plaque on the gate to **719 Windsor Lane**.

Hersey, whose fondness for anagrams is evident in his collection of short stories *Key West Tales*, surely would have appreciated the interplay of "Hersey" and "heresy" in this tribute.

Passover Lane perplexes me. I had assumed from its location that the name had religious significance—only to learn that the Jewish plots are on the other side of the cemetery.

Jameson says that the short street is so named because it "bounces" across Windsor Lane to Angela. Other sources indicate that it is so called because it jumps over or bounces off Windsor Lane. Perhaps logic has no business here, but as I gaze at the map in front of me, I see that, unlike almost everything else in Key West, the cemetery is not rectangular in shape. Passover Street cuts its western corner, turning the cemetery into a lopsided pentagon. Could this enigma of a street name be so dubbed because it passes over what was once cemetery property?

Crazed bicyclists raced up Passover Street with morning milk. Someone blessed himself behind louvers.

—Thomas McGuane, *Panama*

Johnson Lane

Tucked between Windsor and Packer, and running parallel to Truman and Olivia, Johnson Lane is but a block long. While the evidence is circumstantial, it points toward the naming of this short street for Key West's original cookie lady.

Lena Johnson baked cookies and "pulled" candy for a living, and she was most generous with her goods. She let the Boy Scouts use an outbuilding at the rear of her property for their meetings, whereat she treated them to fresh cookies and candy.

In 1922 Scoutmaster Charles Sands, apparently moved by Ms. Johnson's generosity, asked the National Scout Headquarters for permission to christen her their scout mother.

They liked the idea, and thus began the tradition of scout and den mothers nurturing the youth of America.

The first scout mother lived on a narrow byway that ran parallel to Division Street (Truman Avenue). Today, not coincidentally I believe, it is called Johnson Lane.

Carey, Cates, and Catholic Lanes

Carey Lane appears to be a dead-end extension of Angela Street at Margaret. Probably it was named for businessman George H. Carey, ex-sailor and expatriate (from England), who usually sported a high silk hat. Carey, H. L. Ware, and Henry Mulrennan were partners who operated a haberdashery in the Louvre on Front Street. Another Carey, Alicia, was also an entrepreneur. Her line was ice cream. When the mule-drive streetcars extended their routes beyond the corporate limits in the 1890s, she capitalized by opening an ice cream parlor near the terminus.

He brought all the money back to Key West and bought a little shack of a house on Catholic Lane around the corner from Maggie.

—John Leslie, *Blood on the Keys*

Catholic Lane runs off Angela, across from the Catholic sector of the cemetery, which was added to the burial grounds in 1861. Within the same block, off Frances, is **Cates Lane**. Though religious, "Sister" Cates was not a Catholic. For years this devout Baptist held her congregation together by raising money to bring in itinerant preachers. Her persistence paid off:

the Southern Baptist Convention finally put Key West under the aegis of its Home Mission Board, which assigned permanent pastors to minister to the faithful.

Pohalski Village

On the other side, off the western corner of the cemetery, are **Havana Street** and **Pohalski Avenue,** byways that echo the area's once thriving cigar-manufacturing industry. Havana Street, like Havana in north Florida (pronounced "Hay-vana" by the locals), is named for the Cuban city from which such good leaf was once imported (and is now contraband). In the late 1880s, cigar magnate Pincus Pohalski, a transplant from Texas, built a factory and then established an entire village within this block. **Nichols Avenue,** also within the former village, is named for B. C. Nichols, principal of the Sears School at the turn of the century.

Despite its name and location, nearby **Ashe Street** is not connected to the cigar industry. It is named for Thomas J. Ashe, one of Key West's first city engineers. Thomas and wife Geraldine were inseparable in marriage, but as streets they stand apart. **Geraldine Street** is back over on the other side of the island, alongside Petronia.

Newton and Albury Streets

On the Gulf side of White is nestled a quiet residential neighborhood that extends to Eisenhower Drive. Parallel to Angela is **Newton Street.** Definitely not named for Sir Isaac and probably not even for Dr. J. Y. Porter's granddaughter, Jessie Porter Newton, leader of the island's restoration movement until her death in 1979, Newton may simply be an example of how the

British designated towns by just adding a suffix. Indeed this street was located in what was once the newer part of town.

Of **Albury Street** we can be more certain. The Albury clan, starting with first settler Benjamin, established itself on the island early. By the late 1800s, Richard Henry Albury owned some of the Key West's most valuable real estate. His brother, William Henry Albury, built a frill-free Conch house that stands as a prime example of nineteenth-century island architecture. The **Albury House** is located at **730 Southard**.

Pine Street

Jane rented a room in the back of a large Conch house on Pine Street, fifteen minutes from downtown Key West.

—John Leslie, *Damaged Goods*

No doubt, writer John Dos Passos, who lived at **1401 Pine** during the 1930s, made the fifteen-minute walk often. After one nocturnal amble, he arrived at the Hemingways' house and met his future wife, Kate, for the first time. Perhaps it was kismet: "Dos" had, after all, been the one to suggest that "ole Hem" give Key West a try if he was looking for a warm place "to dry out his bones."

Little Streets

The old Dos Passos abode, fifteen minutes from Hem's place.

Eisenhower Drive

His names sum up the man. Dwight D. Eisenhower's boyhood nickname, Ike, stayed with him throughout his life. It reflects an affability that put everyone in his presence at ease, and it lent itself readily to the "I Like Ike" campaign slogan that helped get him elected president twice. Ike's family name, Eisenhower, comes from the German words for "iron striker." Indeed, General Eisenhower had the qualities needed to do the necessary planning and organizing, make the tough decisions, and then execute them without equivocation during both wartime and peacetime.

Born in 1890 into a Quaker family that had emigrated from Germany via Switzerland in 1732, Ike lived in Abilene, Kansas, until he graduated from high school and entered the Military Academy at West Point. As an Army officer he earned steady, but not rapid, promotions. In the 1930s, he served as an assistant to General Douglas MacArthur, military adviser to the Commonwealth of the Philippines, Eisenhower worked under MacArthur for five years, but he was still a junior officer when World War II erupted. In the wartime Army, however, Ike rose rapidly. Days after the Japanese bombed Pearl Harbor, Chief of Staff General George Marshall made Eisenhower the head of the war plans division. By war's end, General Eisenhower was supreme commander of the Allied Expeditionary Forces.

Late into his first term as president, Eisenhower, at the behest of his doctors, visited Key West. They were concerned that he was not recuperating quickly enough from a heart attack and prescribed ten days of relaxation and sunshine. In Key West he was a guest of the U.S. Navy, so he probably stayed at his predecessor's Little White House.

Like the man, his namesake street is direct and unambiguous. From Palm to Truman, Eisenhower Drive runs in a straight line along the shore of Garrison Bight. Before it took on our thirty-fourth president's name, most of this street was known as North Beach Road. The stretch near Truman marked where Salt Pond Road began its meandering path along the edges of an island yet to be reconfigured by landfill.

Gibralter of the Americas

We motor in along the Overseas Highway; we touch down at Meacham Field and step out into the humid subtropics; or, restoring a sense of island to the place, we arrive by sea. Vacationers, tourists, residents, retirees, entrepreneurs, seekers of fortune and fame, we are all hard pressed to imagine that Key West was once a vital link in America's defense and foreign policy, that it was considered our Gibraltar.

In the early 1820s, at the same time Commodore Porter was using "Allenton" as a base of operations to rid the region of pirates that had been bedeviling the sea lanes for centuries, his commander-in-chief was devising policy that had farther-reaching consequences. Global in scope, Monroe's doctrine declared that the United States would stay out of entangling affairs in Europe and, in turn, a status quo would prevail throughout the

Western Hemisphere. Europe could keep its established colonies, but any attempt by European powers to interfere in the Americas would be considered a threat to U.S. national security.

Key West, gateway to the Gulf of Mexico, was strategically positioned to project American military might in defense of the Monroe Doctrine. To this end, Commodore Porter established a Naval presence on the island in 1823, a year after Key West was permanently settled. By 1831 the Army's barracks were in place where Anderson Street once ran. Then, to further bolster our southern defenses (and offenses),two massive forts were conceived, planned, and constructed.

Fort Jefferson

Construction on Ft. Jefferson, 70 miles west of Key West on Garden Key in the Dry Tortugas, was started in 1846. Some twenty years and sixteen million bricks later, this huge hexagon, dubbed by some the Gibraltar of the Gulf, dominated the tiny islands of the Dry Tortugas. Standing fifty high, with eight-foot-thick walls, this structure may be made up of more bricks than any other building in the Western world—and that was one of the problems. Eventually it became apparent that the planners and architects had overlooked something very fundamental. Beneath the weight of those bricks, the fort was slowly sinking. Under the fort's foundation was not, as was believed, solid coral, but a composite of sand, shell, and loose coral. At times like this, the Fates can be most forgiving, it seems. Advances in military technology would soon make the fortification obsolete anyway, and its subsiding foundation would become a matter of only incidental interest.

Ft. Zachary Taylor

St. James and the Wendy finally arrived in the harbor with the crews listening to the melancholy sound of the Fort Taylor regimental band playing "Annie Laurie," which it had recently learned and played at its weekly Saturday concerts for the town.

—Robert N. Macomber, *Point of Honor*

Ft. Jefferson's slightly older, yet smaller and less shapely, sister was also waterlocked. Perched on a rock ledge some four hundred meters offshore, alongside the Straits of Florida, this trapezoidal fortification once commanded all water entry to Key West.

In 1845 construction on the unnamed fort began. As with Ft. Jefferson, brick was imported by ship from Pensacola, and Irish and German masons were recruited from New York and Philadelphia. Slaves, hired out by their Key West owners (or imported by the Union Army during the Civil War), also provided some of the labor. On October 11, 1846, a devastating hurricane struck Key West and wiped out whatever work had been done. Construction was resumed immediately, however, and by 1861 the fort, now christened Ft. Zachary Taylor, was ready for occupancy.

Zachary Taylor was similar to Dwight D. Eisenhower in a couple of respects. Both were military heroes and both won the only office they ever ran for: the U.S. presidency. However, unlike Ike's presidency, Taylor's was short-lived. He died suddenly, just sixteen months into his only term.

Born into a military family in 1784, Taylor was raised in western Virginia, in what later became Kentucky. Like a few other early American presidents, young Taylor had no formal schooling. Home-schooled and tutored for a while, he seemed to learn mostly from his environment, an environment dominated by former Revolutionary War soldiers who had received land grants for their services. Zach and all but one of his four brothers joined the Army.

Distinguishing himself in the War of 1812 and, decades later, against the Black Hawk Indians in Wisconsin, Colonel Taylor was sent to Florida to fight the Seminoles. In late 1837 Taylor's men defeated the Seminoles in the decisive Battle of Lake Okeechobee. Their leader was promoted to brigadier general and given command of all U.S. troops in Florida. In 1845, just as construction of the fort that was to be named for him began, General Taylor was ordered to advance to the Rio Grande and secure our natural boundary with Mexico. During the ensuing Mexican War, Taylor's brilliant battlefield leadership and his daring invasion of northern Mexico caught the nation's attention. At Buena Vista, against superior forces, Taylor emerged with a victory that earned him the nickname "Old Rough and Ready."

On the strength of his military heroics, Taylor was pushed into the national spotlight. The moribund Whig Party (in 1854 the Republican Party would be born of its split) desperately needed a strong presidential candidate and, though inactive, Taylor was a Whig. Expressing doubts about his qualifications, the reluctant candidate agreed to accept his party's nomination and then went on to become the second (and last) Whig president of the United States.

During the War Between the States, Ft. Taylor's importance was measured not in protecting the country from foreign threat but in preserving the Union. As soon as Florida seceded (and Confederates began pilfering the federal arsenals in St. Augustine, Fernandina, and Chattahoochee), Captain James Brannan, the highest ranking officer on Key West, took decisive action. Acting without orders from Washington, he marched his fifty troops stationed at the Army barracks through town, across the causeway that connected Ft. Taylor to the island, and secured it for the Union. Throughout Florida federal troops took similar action. Ft. Clinch at Fernandina, San Marcos at St. Augustine, the federal arsenal at Chattahoochee, and Ft. Jefferson in the Dry Tortugas were all secured in January 1861. And in April, days after the outbreak of actual fighting, Union soldiers reinforced the garrisons at Ft. Pickens on Santa Rosa Island near Pensacola, thus occupying another post deep in enemy territory.

Ft. Taylor, and thus Key West, stayed in Union hands throughout the Civil War. At that time Key West was the largest city in Florida, and its occupation by federal forces was indeed a factor that determined the outcome of the war. Key West was the most strategic point in the underbelly of the Confederacy. In the hands of the federal government, it served as a base of operations for Union forces; conversely, its occupation denied the Confederate states similar use.

The fifty soldiers who secured the fort had four months of provisions and some seventy thousand gallons of water in their cisterns to sustain them. They were prepared for a siege and for possible assault from Confederate sympathizers across the causeway. The assault never came, but reinforcements did. Over in Texas, Major William H. French's Fifth U.S. Artillery was being chased by the Rebels. To avoid surrender, they marched down the Rio Grande to Point Isabel, where they set sail for Ft. Taylor.

Upon arrival, Major French, apparently acting without orders, suspended the writ of habeas corpus in Key West. Inasmuch as the city was already under martial law, French's action was approved by his commander at Ft. Pickens. In a letter of approval dated May 13, 1861, French also received instruction that all troops were to remain in Key West because it was "of paramount importance, and must not be weakened for any contingency service."

Eventually more reinforcements arrived and Ft. Taylor was put to more active use. It served as headquarters for the Eastern Gulf Blockading Squadron. The South, lacking the industrial might of the North, was unable to produce the armaments and munitions needed to wage a successful war. Thus it had to rely on exporting its cotton and other agricultural products and importing military goods and supplies. With a coastline that stretched down the Atlantic and up the Gulf coast, the South had many ports from which to move its goods, and the North would prevail only if it could block this traffic.

The thirty vessels based at Ft. Taylor played an important role in this effort. They were dispatched regularly to intercept and capture blockade runners and Confederate ships at sea. Almost two hundred suspect vessels were impounded at Ft. Taylor, where they rode out the war anchored beneath the mammoth guns that kept watch overhead.

By 1862 some nine hundred men were stationed at Ft. Taylor, where a majority of them contracted yellow fever. The three hundred who died from the disease are commemorated by the memorial obelisk that stands in Clinton Place.

As indicated, once secured and reinforced, the fort played a greater role in the war. Late in the struggle, in the spring of

1865, a force was sent north under the command of Brigadier General John Newton. Its mission was to capture the port at St. Marks and then march on Tallahassee, the only southern capital not in Union hands. Newton's forces landed at the St. Marks lighthouse and proceeded along the St. Marks River, where they were repulsed at Natural Bridge. Thus, Tallahassee was to remain the only Confederate capital not occupied by Yankee troops during the war. And whatever became of General Newton? After his retreat at Natural Bridge, did he return to Key West, where that street in new town was eventually named after him?

At war's end, construction continued on the fort, but not for long. Due to technological advances in weaponry, Ft. Taylor became a sitting duck at water's edge. Rifled cannon could now spit out a projectile that would no longer bounce off thick masonry walls. Spinning, it would dig into the masonry and burrow its way deep before exploding. Ft. Taylor and Ft. Jefferson immediately became obsolete.

During the Spanish-American War and World Wars I and II, Ft. Taylor was reactivated and used temporarily. At some point most of the huge guns, their carriages, and their cannonballs were dumped over the southeast wall and covered with sand and cement. Inadvertently preserved, this trove of Civil War armaments has been only partially excavated and recovered.

For a while Ft. Taylor itself was similarly covered up. To expand the naval base, the area around the causeway was filled in, and the fort was used as a dumping ground for the sludge that had been dredged from the sea bottom. Excavation began in the late 1960s and continued into the 1970s. One of the treasures found beneath the muck was a water desalinization plant capable of turning some seven thousand gallons of sea water into drinking water each day.

The dredging completed, the land filled, the muck removed, Ft. Taylor and what was once sea are now a fifty-acre Florida state park.

The Martello Towers

She was standing with her back against the old Civil War fortress, the West Martello Tower, one foot propped against the brick facade, her tight black skirt hiked up to reveal bare leg. It was a classic pose. . .
—John Leslie, *Killer in Paradise*

The exact origin of the term *martello* is unclear. We know that the first structure bearing the characteristics now associated with Martello towers was built in Corsica, on Cape Mortello. Was this distinctive architecture named for the place or for a Spanish military engineer named Mortello who built the prototype? To further complicate matters, we have the root word *mart-* (derived from Mars, the Roman god of war) in all the Romance languages. In Portuguese and Italian, *martello* means "hammer," as does *martella* in Spanish and *martel* in French.

Whatever the origin of the term, this type of eighteenth-century fortification was capable of dishing out—and taking— a considerable pounding. In 1794 the British tried to land an invading force of fourteen hundred on Corsica. Defended by only a couple of cannons and a handful of troops, the tower absorbed considerable hammering and was holding its own until a lucky hot shot landed within and ignited some combustible rubble.

Duly impressed, when threatened by invasion from

Napoleon's French empire, the British copied the Corsican design and erected a string of their own Martello towers along the Irish and Kentish coasts of the British Isles. The French never invaded, so these coastal defenses never withstood the test of fire. The British must have had great faith in their purloined design, though; they built others in their New World, in Nova Scotia, New Brunswick, and Kingston, Canada.

The architecture of a Martello tower is a rather sophisticated combination of arches, piers, groins, and other masonry. But basically the design is one of a central tower or citadel within an outer tower. The central tower is a square, fifty-six feet to a side at its base and tapering gradually as it rises to a height of thirty-six feet. Its walls are eight feet thick on the seaward side and five feet solid landside. The outer tower is lower and forms a formidable perimeter that must first be penetrated if the fortress is to fall. Galleries and storehouses are located within the first line of defense, between the citadel and the outer walls. In a completed tower, this space would be covered by a roof supported by a network of arches and barrel vaults. Topside would sit the heavy guns.

The only access to a completed tower would be over the ramparts and across a drawbridge. Invaders who might penetrate the perimeter would probably be greeted with a hail of hot pitch. Atop the central tower, made accessible by a narrow circular stairway, were openings on each side whence the defenders could rain down their punishment.

The girdle of towers proposed for Key West was to work in tandem with Ft. Taylor. Original plans called for four towers: the two existing ones, another on nearby Stock Island, and the fourth on Fleming Key to the north. Sites for fortifications were identified in 1845, the same year that construction started on Ft. Taylor. Construction on the towers was, however, delayed until the late 1850s and never begun at the Stock Island and Fleming Key sites.

The purpose of the Ft. Taylor Advanced Battery was to protect the land side of Ft. Taylor from invasion. To land an invading force successfully, offshore vessels would have to lay down a covering field of fire. The East and West Martello Towers are positioned so that they can interdict this firepower from gunboats. To assure that both towers could be adequately supplied and stocked with munitions, a narrow gauge railroad was built from Ft. Taylor to the nearest tower and then onward to East Martello Tower a few miles away.

At the outbreak of the Civil War, construction of the towers stopped. (During the war, Union forces got the most use from the West Tower, which they used for target practice.) After the war, construction was resumed, but only briefly. Like their parent fort, the once impregnable Martello Towers were rendered obsolete by the threat of rifled cannon shot.

Since then they have been put to other uses. In 1951 the Key West Art and Historical Society moved into East Martello Tower, where it maintains an art gallery and a museum dedicated to Key West history. The West Tower was once put to more practical use. For years cattle imported from Punta Rassa near Ft. Myers were corralled in the battered structure before being slaughtered on a nearby beach. Now the Key West Garden Club calls West Martello Tower home and welcomes all within its flora-filled walls.

Higgs Memorial Beach

At Clarence J. Higgs Memorial Beach, I walked out the plank dock. It goes out . . . and then stops at the ruins of an older dock. . . .
—Thomas McGuane, *Panama*

The West Martello Tower may not be the finest example of its unique architecture in the western world. (The East Tower has that distinction.) It does, however, have other virtues. Besides being home to the Garden Club, it sits nicely between two beaches.

For decades the beach to the west of the tower was called County Beach. As indicated above, it has been renamed in memory of Clarence Higgs, former mayor of Key West.

At **Higgs Beach** there is imported sand and shallow water just deep enough for swimming. There are also sheltered picnic tables, restrooms, an outdoor shower, and a playground for kids. The sidewalk provides ample space for biking, skating, and

140

dodging those on roller blades.

But once a year Higgs Beach steps beyond its quotidian routine. On that summer day, it provides a venue for those who wish to test themselves against the sea and its currents. The beach becomes the starting point for athletes who won't touch land again until they swim the twelve miles around the island. Some swimmers race, others just like the challenge.

It would be just like her to go and drown herself at Higgs Beach before he could do it. Then when he did, he would be part of a trend.
—Alison Lurie, *The Last Resort*

On the other side of West Martello Tower is a stretch of beach that has been known by many names. Fortunately, no name was attached to its use as an abattoir, where the cattle shipped from Punta Rassa and corralled in the nearby tower were slaughtered. Later the beach was upgraded slightly to serve as a city dump. Years after this land (mis)use was stopped, islanders were fond of digging up what they could of the buried refuse. Many old bottles were found beneath the sand, hence the name Bottle Beach. During the Depression the government got involved. As part of a Federal Emergency Relief Administration project, the area was given a makeover to attract tourists. Palm-thatched cabanas were erected, and what was once a dump became **Rest Beach**, the name we hear most often today.

He also told me that I was cavorting in the sand at Rest Beach at three in the morning. I told him he'd made this up. He said, "You cut your foot on a Doctor Pepper bottle."

—Thomas McGuane, *Panama*

Recently it has come to light that those who cavort at the beach may be doing so on sacred ground. Well before the area served the functions mentioned above, it was a burial ground. The newly erected historical marker across from the tower spells it out.

AFRICAN CEMETERY AT HIGGS BEACH
Near this site lie the remains of 294 African men,
women, and children. . . .

And on it goes to tell the story of the U.S. Navy rescue of some fourteen hundred enslaved souls who were bound for a life of servitude in Cuba. They were brought to Key West, where they stayed for three months. Most were repatriated to Africa, but, as indicated above, almost three hundred would never return. Notwithstanding what the marker indicates, to date nine graves have been unearthed on the Rest Beach (not Higgs) side of the tower. It was there, in a fifteen-hundred-square-foot area that has been enclosed by chain-link fence, that the remains of some of the Africans were uncovered.

Truman Avenue

"Out on the other end of town," said Professor MacWalsey. "Past the Park. Down the street from the place where they sell mullets."

"That's the Rocky Road," the driver said.

"Yes," said Professor MacWalsey. . . . As they turned on to the worn white coral of the Rocky Road. . . .

—Ernest Hemingway, *To Have and Have Not*

As we saw a few pages back, when Union troops that were garrisoned at the Army barracks made their nighttime move to secure Ft. Taylor, they marched through town to the causeway, about a mile away. To avoid having to continually traverse an island teeming with Confederate sympathizers, General John M. Brannan, commanding officer at the Army post, hacked out a slightly longer route to the fort.

This road began about a thousand feet from the garrison and cut straight across the key. Named presumably for the general (by coincidence, as we saw earlier, Captain James M. Brannan led the march to secure Ft. Taylor), Brannan Road was rough going. Although trees were felled and brush whacked, the road was still strewn with so much coral rock that islanders called it Rocky Road. This moniker was even pronounced phonetically as *Rokirro* by the Spanish-speaking residents. Officially though, it was either Brannan or, as specified on 1870s deeds, Military Road. Later this multi-named road was called Division Street, because it formed the dividing line between Old Town and the sparsely populated land to the east.

In 1868 a group of French Canadian nuns, the Sisters of the Holy Name of Jesus and Mary, arrived in Key West, probably at the behest of their fellow countrymen. The Reverend Father LaRocque was pastor of St. Mary, Star of the Sea, Church; Father Bernier was his assistant. The nuns moved into a frame house across from the lighthouse, at the junction of Whitehead and Division, and opened a school for white girls. By 1875 they had started schools for white boys (1869), Spanish-speaking Cuban girls (1873), and colored girls, and hired a lay teacher named I. Cappick, to teach the boys. (Almost a century later, one of his descendants, Marie Cappick, would be writing extensively about the history of Key West.)

With so many students to teach, the good Sisters needed more room. A suitable site was found, an architect commissioned, and work on a convent cum schoolhouse began in 1875. William Kerr (1836–1911), whose credits include City Hall, the Court House, the "Old Stone" Methodist Church, the U.S. Customs House, and his residence at **410 Simonton**, designed the Convent of Mary Immaculate. Located mid-island near the corner of Windsor and Division (Tract 12), the stately structure was built with limestone quarried from the island. Reportedly, even the nuns pitched in to construct their future home. True to their origins, these French Canadians had Kerr affect a Second-Empire architectural style.

Years later, the nuns also pitched in to give U.S. Army Hospital corpsmen a hand in treating some of the sick and wounded returning from the Spanish-American War in Cuba. When some became many, Sister Superior offered the convent and other buildings to Captain W.T. Sampson, commander of U.S. Naval Forces, North Atlantic Station. Her offer was accepted and parts of the buildings converted into hospital wards for the five hundred convalescing soldiers. Many decades later, in 1960, the Second Empire met the modern age. The convent was demolished, and a more functional, concrete structure was erected in its place.

Soon after the war, on September 20, 1901, the Catholic Church that was home to the French Canadian nuns was gutted by fire. By then, Father LaRocque was back in Quebec, where he was eventually consecrated bishop of Sherbrooke. His successor began holding services in a sick bay built by the U.S. government on convent grounds. He must have liked the location, for it was decided that the new church would move from "church central" near St. Paul's on Duval and be built on the same grounds as the Convent of Mary Immaculate. Kerr, who designed the convent, was commissioned to draw up plans for the church.

Construction started in February 1904. On August 20, 1905, the Right Reverend W. J. Kenny, bishop of St. Augustine, dedicated a new Church of St. Mary, Star of the Sea. Among St. Mary's more celebrated parishioners were Ernest and Pauline Hemingway. Ernest, a Congregationalist in his youth, had converted to Catholicism before his marriage to Pauline.

On November 23, 1948, with Key West Mayor Maitland Adams presiding at the dedication, Division Street underwent yet another name change: it became Truman Avenue.

They were on Truman Avenue now, rolling past the Catholic Church.

—Burt Hirschfeld, *Key West*

President Harry S. Truman, like his successor Dwight D. Eisenhower, was a Midwesterner. Born on a farm in 1884, Truman spent his early adulthood in a succession of jobs. By twenty-two he had been a timekeeper for the Santa Fe Railroad in Kansas City, a newspaper wrapper for the *Kansas City Star*, a bank clerk, and a bookkeeper. When his dad died, he returned to the family farm.

Despite poor eyesight, Truman joined the Army when the United States entered World War I. As a field artillery officer, he saw action at the Argonne Forest in France. After the war he returned to Missouri, where he went into partnership with a fellow veteran. They opened a men's clothing store in Kansas City. As a haberdasher, Truman simply did not measure up. At the maturing age of thirty-seven, he had yet to establish himself in any career.

Under the tutelage of Democratic Party boss "Big Tom"

Pendergast, Truman got started in politics. From his appointment to the misnamed office of presiding judge (actually overseer of Jackson County's business affairs, primarily its road building), Truman rose to his country's highest political office. There, President Truman made a decision we hope no other leader will be pressed to make: he ordered that the only two atomic bombs in our arsenal be dropped on Japan—and World War II came to an early end.

A year later, Truman began retreating to the naval station in Key West for rest and relaxation. Quarters A & B, built in 1890 to house the naval commandant and his paymaster, and used later for VIPs, were turned into the Little White House. This spacious getaway was home to Truman during his working vacations on the island. (Taft, Coolidge, Franklin Roosevelt, and Kennedy took day trips to Key West, but only Truman and Eisenhower stayed overnight.)

A common man with a common touch, Truman distinguished himself in common pursuits. He read and he exercised. His daily routine included a long, brisk walk at military pace (120 steps to a minute, 4 mph), followed by various aerobic and resistance exercises, and then a swim. Key West proved to be the perfect winter setting for his regimen.

Truman's other passion was reading. Never schooled beyond the secondary level, Truman was largely self-taught. His interest in history proved to be the ideal subject to prepare him for his presidency. Well grounded, Truman set the stage for the postwar, cold-war politics that followed his two terms in office.

They put me in a southern built house with "galleries" all around, upstairs and down. It was the commandant's house—at present there is no commandant—so I did not "rank" anyone out of his house.
—Harry S. Truman, "Letter to His Mother and Sister"

More Little Streets

Southernmost point it is called, mile zero. Last hope for star-crossed creatures dreaming in tropical pastures at the end of the American road.

—Thomas Sanchez, *Mile Zero*

The following section will cover an area bounded by Howe on the fort side of the island, George Street two miles away, Truman Avenue, and Hawk Channel on the Atlantic Ocean side. This is as large a sector as covered heretofore.

Moving away from Old Town, we find that many streets bear names of little or no historic interest. Similarly, many either have names of obvious origin or have been given "first" names that were of significance only to the namer and some insiders. Thus, as we begin to cover more ground, I cover fewer pages with print.

Howe Street

Howe Street is probably named for the Charles Howe who obtained controlling interest in the LaFayette Salt Company in the early 1840s. His partners were Adam Gordon, F. A. Browne, and William H. Wall, who had purchased the company from Simonton and other absentee stockholders living in Mobile and New Orleans. After the devastating hurricane of 1846, Howe became sole proprietor, and things began panning out. In 1850 he produced a crop of some thirty-five thousand bushels of salt. This output encouraged him to expand his operation. He bought the Whitehead portion of the pond, abandoned, as you may recall, by Richard Fitzpatrick when he moved to Miami. Between 1861 and 1869, Howe, presumably a Union supporter, served as collector of customs in Yankee-controlled Key West.

Howe's origins are unclear. There was a Charles Howe of Indian Key, who owned Key Vaca (largest settlement outside Key West in the 1830s). This Howe was also Indian Key's inspector of customs and postmaster, as well as a partner of Dr. Henry Perrine. (Perrine founded the Tropical Plant Company, an enterprise that tried unsuccessfully to grow Sea Island, Georgia, cotton and mulberry plants for the production of raw silk.)

The Howes of Indian Key had five children, all of whom escaped with their mother and father during the Indian massacre on Indian Key in 1840. (Dr. Perrine did not.) Perhaps they relocated to the sanctuary of Key West, where Howe senior or a namesake son went into the salt business.

Five Mysterious Ladies

Running perpendicular to Howe and parallel to Truman are **Julia, Virginia, Amelia, Catherine,** and **Louisa Streets.** The origins of these street names remain a mystery. Were they wives, daughters, or mothers of developers? Lady friends of mapmakers or postmasters charged with designating where the mail should go? Were they favorite aunts or teachers of some fire chief who put their names on rocky paths so his firefighters would know where to go? Is Virginia named for a woman or for the state? As we move across a modern Key West, more of these quandaries will surface.

Virginia Street

The wild symptoms she'd had while reading the letter had faded by the time she had changed, and as she drove to Virginia Street, all she felt was a hard lump in her stomach.

—John Hersey, "Fantasy Fest"

Down Virginia, over a mile from its Howe Street origin, stands a condominium that was once home to cigar magnate Eduardo Hidalgo-Gato and family. In 1869 Gato, just a few steps ahead of the authorities, fled Cuba to avoid being captured for aiding the rebels during the Ten Years' War. After attempting to start a cigar factory in New York City, this entrepreneur relocated to Key West in 1874, where he became the first Cuban to own a factory.

Originally his home was not located at **1209 Virginia**, near its intersection with White; it stood a few blocks over at the corner of Division Street and Salt Pond Road, in what is

Bayview Park today. Even before the two-story house was moved in 1919, Gato had loaned it to a committee of civic-minded women who converted it into **Casa del Pobre, Mercedes Hospital**, a charity infirmary that was named in honor of Gato's wife.

Catherine Street

If awards are ever given for Key West gate art, the **Hepburn House** at **310-12 Catherine** will be a contender. A colorful, flower-topped sign suggestive of the owner's playfulness is nicely positioned beneath an archway covered with foliage. A delight to the eye. A tickle to our whimsy.

At the **foot of Catherine, where it intersects Howe,** is **Nelson English Park**. It is named for former postmaster Nelson

Katherine would be amused.

F. English, whose real claim to fame was his role as treasurer for the 1870s Key West Coronet Band, which led many a soul to their resting places in City Cemetery.

Farther down Catherine is an area once known as *Barrio de Gato*. Built in the late 1800s, Eduardo Gato's factory served as an anchor for this neighborhood bounded by Duval, Simonton, Amelia, and Catherine. Here, his cigar makers lived, worked, and shopped. In 1917 his factory burned to the ground. As we have seen in the entry about Simonton, it was replaced by a concrete structure that was converted into a Navy commissary when the cigar industry closed shop in Key West.

Still farther down, **at Grinnell**, is another building that was once a cigar factory. The **Armas de Oro cigar factory** was built in 1906, between the industry's peak years of 1890 and 1911, when over one hundred million cigars were produced and exported annually. Eventually Key West lost its status as Florida's top cigar producer to Tampa. In 1896 Vicente Martinez Ybor was persuaded by a delegation from Tampa to relocate there after a fire destroyed his Key West operation. He was but the first to move. Solicitation of other producers, coupled with labor squabbles in Key West, led to an exodus of the industry to what is known as Ybor City today.

South Street

There's a South Street, of course. A southernmost beach.
                                        —Burt Hirschfeld, *Key West*

South Street got its name before Hawaii became our fiftieth state, when it was the southernmost street in the United States.

Replica of a nun-buoy channel marker.

It begins at its junction with Whitehead and the Southernmost Point (that concrete buoy) and runs all the way to George Street, the outer boundary of this section of Little Streets.

Next to the Southernmost Point, at **400 South Street**, we find the **Thelma Strabel House**, the southernmost house on the island. It was built in 1940, perhaps purchased with the royalties from her book and its silver screen adaptation. Ms. Strabel wrote *Reap the Wild Wind*, a story about Key West wrecking in the early days. The novel was first serialized by the *Saturday Evening Post* and then released in book form. The 1944 edition has an introduction by Cecil B. DeMille, who directed the film version. The movie featured established starlet Susan Hayward and a cast of young actors (Ray Milland, John Wayne, and Robert Preston) who would do quite well in Hollywood.

Across the street and down a block, at the **corner of Duval**

and South, is the **Southernmost Point Guesthouse,** circa 1885. Originally this Victorian structure was directly across Duval. Its owner, E. H. Gato Jr., son of the cigar magnate, had it moved to its present location. It seems that the westbound sun heated up his porch and blinded his guests to the extent that socializing became difficult, so he simply moved and repositioned the house.

A block away, next to La Mer Hotel, is the **Dewey House,** once a home-away-from-home for pragmatist philosopher and educator John Dewey. In the autumn of his life, Dewey enjoyed the warm winters of this subtropical island.

Much farther down is the site of yet another former residence of the Hemingways. Between April 1928, when they first visited, and 1931, when they bought the old Tift mansion on Whitehead, Ernest and Pauline visited Key West a number of times. In 1929 they rented at **1100 South Street.** There Ernest completed work on *A Farewell to Arms.* It was also there that the Hemingways received a peculiar parcel from his mother: a chocolate cake and the pistol that Papa's father had killed himself with. Harbinger of things to come, tragic to say.

Washington, running parallel to South, must be named for our first president, George. It runs between Vernon Avenue and George Street. Is this coincidence, or is Vernon named in reference to Washington's Virginia home, Mt. Vernon, and George for his given name?

He turned into Vernon Street, killed his headlights and rolled silently along. . . . He paused behind the structure that used to be Louis' Backyard. . . .

—Burt Hirschfeld, *Key West*

Waddell Avenue

Crossing Vernon and then running a short three blocks from its Dog Beach base to Reynolds Street is Waddell Avenue. James A. Waddell was mayor of Key West for a couple of terms in the late 1800s. It was as a businessman, however, that Waddell inadvertently made his most lasting mark.

In 1889 the Merchants' Protective Association was organized to protect established island merchants from interlopers, mostly street peddlers, who were encroaching on their territory. William Curry was the association's first president, Waddell his successor. Under Waddell's tutelage the city charter was amended so that an occupational license tax of $1,000 could be levied on each peddler. Forced to pay up or quit peddling, many simply opened their own stores, prospered, and became stalwarts of society. Some might even have streets named after them.

Where **Waddell and Vernon** meet is the popular gourmet restaurant **Louie's Backyard**, whose backyard is a sweep of Hawk Channel and the Straits of Florida (its side yard, postage-stamp-sized Dog [or Cable] Beach). Next to Louie's is a former residence of singer Jimmy Buffett. Before stardom propelled him into nicer digs, he rented a modest apartment on Waddell. No longer modest, the renovated two-story is now part of the Coconut Beach Resort. So exclusive that it no longer uses a street address, **Coconut Beach A** marks the spot where the balladeer began wasting away in Margaritaville.

Echeverria turned the next corner and headed toward Louie's Backyard and the Reach, a shady street that was rank with mildew and expensive garbage.

—James W. Hall, *Red Sky at Night*

Seminole Avenue, a short couple of blocks starting at ocean's edge and running slightly inland to conform to the island's grid system of streets, is named for that amalgam of Indian tribes that ended up in Florida. Made up mostly of Creeks and Oconees from Georgia and Alabama, the Seminoles first settled in an empty north Florida. Within decades though, they expanded south and established themselves where the Calusa and other indigenous tribes were no match for their martial prowess.

When poet and Mrs. Robert Frost first visited Key West in the winter of 1934–35, they stayed at 707 Seminole (which is no longer there). Later, like Buffett, they moved on up, to a much nicer dwelling, one we will visit soon.

At the **end of Seminole**, tucked in between water's edge and the tony Coconut Beach Resort, is the **John and Mary Spottswood Waterfront Park**. Dedicated in 2002, this small park is a great place to sea gaze, especially at dawn when the day's earliest light drenches a nearby pier in unearthly colors. An interpretive sign lets the viewer know that beneath the surface is the **Key West Marine Park**, a public underwater expanse that has been reserved to protect the seabed and what remains of its coral. It stretches from the end of Duval Street to the White Street Pier. Part of the park has been roped and buoyed off for swimming and snorkeling.

State Senator John Maloney Spottswood (1920–1975) was a political fixture in Key West for years. He is buried alongside his wife Mary (1923–1996) in the City Cemetery.

Reynolds Street

By the time I got to Reynolds I was in tears. I went down to the park and crossed over to Astro City.

—Thomas McGuane, *Panama*

Reynolds Street originates at United and cuts through South, Washington, Waddell, and Seminole on its way to the sea. It is named for George W. Reynolds, clerk of the circuit court from 1893 to 1905. Perhaps of more interest than George are his mother and mother-in-law.

His mother emigrated from farmlands along the German portion of the long Rhine River. En route to New Orleans, she was shipwrecked near Key West. Like Mrs. George Carey, she became one of the "German brides" who remained on the key.

Reynolds' wife's mom, Drucila Duke, hailed from Cape Florida on Key Biscayne, where her dad was the lighthouse keeper. About the time of the Seminole massacre at Indian Key, Cape Florida was also attacked. Residents abandoned their homes to the Indians and took refuge in the top of the light-house, accessible only by an interior spiral staircase. Undeterred, the Seminoles tried to burn and smoke them out. They were saved by the arrival of a revenue cutter. Years after her harrowing escape, Ms. Duke married Captain Courtland Williams and they begat the daughter whose husband this street is named after.

The end of Reynolds Street marks the beginning of the **Reynolds Street Pier**, which, along with the West Martello Tower, brackets Higgs Beach.

Von Phister Street

A result of this prosperity . . . was that . . . Consuelo's father inherited the bakery and came to own a big house on Von Phister, which had a bright Florida room rimmed with crinkled-glass jalousies.

—John Hersey, "The Two Lives of Consuelo Castanon"

Running off Reynolds through to George is Von Phister Street. There were two William Von Phisters, both buried in the City Cemetery. The Von Phister who lived from 1807 to 1850 was a grocer who owned a store where the Green Parrot stands today (corner of Whitehead and Southard). This Von Phister was also one of the island's first real estate brokers. He and Fred Filer were responsible for dividing up much of the island into parcels and lots. The other Von Phister, apparently his son, was more involved in civic and political affairs.

Von Phister the Younger was elected magistrate in 1860. When the lawmakers in Tallahassee passed the ordinance of secession in January 1861, however, he refused to serve. After the Union troops were firmly in control, Major French, commander of Ft. Taylor, summoned Von Phister and induced him to serve. Later Von Phister became a member of the Union Volunteer Corps of Key West. Apparently his Yankee leanings did not hurt him politically. During Reconstruction he served as county commissioner for a number of terms.

1011 Von Phister was once home to writer Tom McGuane. This concrete-block, suburban-styled house was built in 1940 for Jessie Porter Newton (Dr. Porter's grandchild) by her second husband when McGuane was still toddling about. Decades later, when McGuane purchased the house, he was married to Portia Rebecca Crockett, a descendant of Congressman Davy Crockett, who made his last stand at the Alamo with Jim Bowie and Jim Travis. While living on Von Phister, McGuane finished *The Bushwhacked Piano* and wrote *Ninety-Two in the Shade*. He was also quite busy on the domestic front: he went through a divorce, an affair with actress Elizabeth Ashley, a marriage to actress Margot Kidder, another divorce, and then another marriage, this one to Laurie Buffett, ex-wife of buddy Peter Fonda and sister of struggling pop singer Jimmy Buffett, who was wasting away over on Waddell Street. In turn, Fonda married McGuane's ex-, Becky Crockett, and bought the Von Phister house from him. It came complete with the stained-glass upper window that McGuane had installed. In honor of his featured creatures in *The Bushwhacked Piano*, the artwork depicts a bat against a kaleidoscopic background. The sixties and early seventies were indeed busy, heady times.

More Little Streets

Seminary Street

"Then a couple we'd met at MacDowell who had a house down on Seminary Street lent it to us for the off season, so we came to Key West. And Lorin really dug it."

—Alison Lurie, *The Truth about Lorin Jones*

In the eighteenth century, the term "seminary" did not necessarily connote an institution dedicated to the training and nurturing of young men for the priesthood. A seminary was simply a school or institute of higher learning. For example, when it was founded in 1851, the University of Florida was called the East Florida Seminary, and rival Florida State University, even before it became Florida State College for Women, was the West Florida Seminary.

Seminary Street is so named because it was the final site of Ruth Hargrove Seminary, a Methodist school. The Hargrove Seminary opened in 1890 near the lighthouse, perhaps in the same building used by the nuns before they moved into their new convent. Its next move was past the convent to what was the Gato residence at the end of Division Street near North Beach. Meanwhile, construction on a permanent home for the institute was underway on United (which runs parallel to Seminary). Completed in 1901, the school immediately began to grow. By 1911 so much additional land had been purchased for the thriving school that it occupied around three acres, some of it now fronting the street that came to be known as Seminary.

As with many of the island's streets, there is also a literary connection here. Hemingway's friends, Charles and Lorine Thompson, had moved from their home on Fleming to a spacious, rambling place at **1314 Seminary**. The Thompsons had been such good friends of the Hemingways that Charles joined Ernest and Pauline in 1933, when they went to East Africa on safari. Apparently their friendship was strong enough to survive the Hemingway divorce, Ernest's subsequent marriages to Martha and Mary, and his living in Cuba. More than thirty years after they first met, we find Papa visiting the Thompsons on his last trip to Key West. A year later, Charles would be attending Hemingway's funeral in Ketchum, Idaho.

When Charles died in 1978, the walls of his Seminary Street abode were still adorned with the heads of game he had bagged while on safari with the Hemingways. In March of 2004 the home was on the market. According to its owner of twenty years, the game trophies and other Hemingway memorabilia were still in place and would remain with the house when it was sold.

Whalton Street

Whalton Street runs a half dozen blocks between Seminary and Casa Marina Court. Whalton is a name that reaches back to the beginnings of an anglicized Key West. Joseph C. Whalton and family were among the first permanent settlers on the island. He and Captain Francis Watlington founded the Sons of Temperance, which tempered the drinking habits of islanders from 1845 to 1862. Joseph was the son of the ill-fated John W. Whalton, keeper of the Carysfort Reef lightship.

Besides maintaining the lightship, John tended a small garden on Key Largo. Three years before the Indian Key Massacre, he and a crewman were ambushed and killed by a band of Indians when they went ashore to gather firewood. At the time, his family was living in Key West. The street, however, is probably not named for one of the key's pioneers, but for someone with more official status. Beverly B. Whalton was elected judge of the county court in 1900; he served until his death in 1910.

That afternoon, the Muggers of United Street, as they'd come to be known, were captured. The ladies . . . both lesbians . . . took the Muggers of United Street out with dispatch.

—Burt Hirschfeld, *Key West*

On the other side of Seminary, between United and beyond Truman to Olivia, is Packer Street. The Packers were a New England merchant family that relocated to Key West. Because of their origins, there is a good possibility that their name was really Parker, which the Bostonian tongue rendered *pah-kuh* and the islander ear heard as Packer. However she spelled her last name, Josephine P. owned a lot of property in this area, and Packer Street is named after her. Many Latinos live in this neighborhood, which is home to the popular Cuban eatery **El Siboney (900 Catherine)**.

They usually ate in one of two or three places, chosen for economy. . .and privacy. . . . The Cuban restaurant, El Siboney, on the corner of Catherine and Margaret was Jimenez's favorite.

—John Leslie, *Killer in Paradise*

Watson Street

A half block beyond Packer, toward Garrison Bight, is Grinnell Street, which originated in Old Town and continued on through when this side of Division (Truman) was developed. On the other side of Grinnell is Watson Street. Like Parker, it also runs between Olivia and United. There are a number of Watsons for whom these four blocks could have been named. The most adventuresome of the candidates has to be Robert.

Robert Watson was a dedicated Southerner who, along with Alfred Lowe and William Sawyer, stowed away aboard an English schooner to escape Yankee-infested Key West during the Civil War. They disembarked in Nassau and then hitched back to Cape Florida, whence they hiked up to Jupiter Light. Continuing on to New Smyrna by boat, they disembarked again and walked inland to Enterprise on the St. Johns River. There they boarded a steamer that got them to Jacksonville and then onward, back down the Atlantic coast and into the Gulf to Tampa, where they enlisted in the Seventh Florida Regiment.

Another contender for the honor is George G. Watson, a member of the consortium that received, in 1885, the franchise from the Florida Legislature to operate a streetcar line outside the corporate limits of Key West. Consortium member Eduardo Gato financed the operation and ran it as a private concern. For horsepower, the streetcars used mules.

In the **1000 block** of Watson Street, on the odd-numbered side, is a warren of cottages and compounds. Laurence Shames, one of the writers whose words have been excerpted to liven up these pages, lived in one of the compounds while absorbing the color and cadence of the island that flavor his work so well.

They proceeded along Truman Avenue, down Watson and across United, in a deliberate geriatric shuffle, as if the sidewalk underfoot were the enemy.

—Burt Hirschfeld, *Key West*

Varela Street

Varela is a common enough Hispanic surname. Thus, my assumption that the three blocks between Truman and United are named for Felix Francisco Jose Maria de la Concepcion Varela y Morales may seem a leap of faith to some. After all, my research turned up no links to a Father or Doctor Varela. But, over at 909 Fleming, there is a Masonic temple that was organized in 1868 and named Dr. Felix Varela Lodge No. 64, and in the City Cemetery there is a crypt that appears to hold the remains of Dr. Varela, as well as those of lodge members.

Upon closer inspection, however, you will see that the vault of Dr. Varela differs from the others. Indeed, it bears his name, but there are no birth and death dates, just the nomenclature of the Masonic chapter named after him. So, just who was this man whose stature inspired others to name their organization in his honor and inter their dead alongside his empty vault? A trip to the San Carlos Institute on Duval cleared up the mystery.

A bust of Padre Verela stands beneath the stairs inside the institute. Behind it, on the wall, is a poster of an enlarged postage stamp that bears his visage. Good enough, but were the saintly priest and the good doctor one and the same? It seems they were.

Dr. Felix Varela Lodge.

Priest, scholar, reformer, soon to be a saint?

Varela was a true Renaissance man, both saintly and secular, academic and streetwise. Born in Havana and raised in Spanish St. Augustine, he returned to Havana to become both a priest and a professor. An early advocate of independence for Cuba, Varela was sentenced to death by the Spanish Crown. He escaped and eventually made his way to New York City, where he founded Transfiguration Church in Chinatown. Thus he became the social reformer who, a century and a half later, would be honored by postal authorities for ministering to the downtrodden immigrants of nineteenth-century New York.

Like most funereal inscriptions, the one beneath his bust sums it all up, but really tells us nothing of the man whose life was bracketed by the dates.

*Born in Cuba in 1788; died and buried in
St. Augustine in 1853.*

Eliza Street

On the other side of White, running through to Leon, is Eliza Street, named for Eliza Gordon, who was either the wife or daughter of Adam Gordon. Gordon, a prominent lawyer, was district attorney in 1834, collector of customs from 1838 to 1845, and first judge of probate court for a short time. He was also something of an entrepreneur. In 1835 he, F. A. Brown, and William H. Wall were majority stockholders in the Lafayette Salt Company, which was eventually controlled by Charles Howe, whom we met earlier. Gordon was also a major promoter of a subdivision at the west end of the island. At some point, though, he left Key West and moved to Connecticut. Of the two possible Elizas, all we know, thanks to Jefferson Browne, is that Mrs. Gordon was "a woman of sterling qualities" and her daughter a girl of "sweet disposition" when she left the island with her parents.

Duncan Street

Duncan Street runs parallel to Eliza, but goes through to George. It was named for B. M. Duncan, the director of the Overseas Highway, the road that made access to Key West easy, in effect turning the island into a peninsula connected to the mainland. Before the highway was completed in 1938, access by land was either by rail or by car via the ferries that linked roads on some keys. The Labor Day Hurricane of 1935 bypassed Key West, but slammed into the Middle and Upper Keys, killing hundreds and washing out some twenty miles of rail and rail bed. Already in financial straits, the Flagler system chose to sell its interest to the federal government. Using track bed that had not been washed away, the railway bridges, and whatever else remained intact of the right-of-way, Duncan's crews linked Key West to Ft. Kent, Maine, twenty-two hundred miles away.

Playwright Tennessee Williams lived on Duncan Street for some thirty years. Years before Williams purchased it in 1949, his home at **1431** had been moved from Old Town to the very outskirts of Key West. While he lived and worked on Duncan, the neighborhood grew up around and beyond him. Here, in the studio he had built out back next to his beloved swimming pool, Williams did much of his best work.

More Little Streets

Jose Marti Boulevard

This "boulevard" is as much a misnomer as some of those "streets" we encountered in Old Town that ran for a few hundred feet. Jose Marti Boulevard runs for one block along Bayview Park. Most probably this stretch of road was so designated because a bust of the Cuban revolutionary stands in the park. Erected by the Cuban government, it was dedicated and presented in 1937.

José Julian Martí made Key West his base for exporting revolution to Cuba, and, as mentioned in the section on Duval Street, the house now named the La Te Da provided a venue for spreading his revolutionary zeal. A visionary of many talents and strong convictions, he died young, apparently doing what he was destined to do.

Bayview Park is, of course, named for its proximity to Garrison Bight. At one time, cigar manufacturer and philanthropist Eduardo H. Gato owned this two-square block of open space. After he moved Mercedes Hospital off his premises to Virginia Street, he deeded the property to the city to be used as a public park.

Jose Marti Boulevard occupies what would be the logical extension of Leon Street (named, I assume, for Ponce de León, the first Westerner to spot the Keys and explore Florida). Only a block long, Marti Boulevard begins at the intersection of streets named for three successive U.S. presidents, Roosevelt, Truman, and Eisenhower; it ends at Virginia, where Leon begins and runs all the way to Atlantic Boulevard.

Casa Marina

How was I to have an occasion at the Casa Marina, which had not been operating for a quarter century, when the grass grew to one's waist? . . .

—Thomas McGuane, *Panama*

The **Casa Marina** dominates the right angle that is formed by Seminole Avenue, Reynolds Street, and a thousand feet of shoreline. This "House of the Sea" marks the last link in the Flagler chain of luxury hotels that dot Florida's East Coast. Henry Flagler died in 1913, five years before construction began on his Key West conception. Carrère and Hastings, the same architectural firm that designed Flagler's initial extravaganza, the Ponce de Leon in St. Augustine, put together the blueprints for the Casa Marina. By 1921 the three-wing, three-story, two-hundred-room hotel was finished. Total cost: $350,000.

The hotel, whose architecture has been variously described as Mediterranean, semi-Moorish, and Spanish Renaissance, was home to a couple of important literary figures in the 1930s and 1940s. Poet Robert Frost moved in from a humbler abode across the way (707 Seminole) at about the same time fellow poet Wallace Stevens took up winter residence there in 1934.

Stevens, by profession an insurance executive from Hartford, Connecticut, had been visiting Key West irregularly since the early 1920s. No doubt he drew deeply on his subtropical surroundings for inspiration. "O Florida Venereal Soil" speaks poignantly of the vivacity Stevens felt on the island. And "The Idea of Order at Key West," a Tennessee Williams favorite, was included in Stevens's *Ideas of Order*, a collection of poems. (Indeed, Williams's fondness of the poem was so well known that it was recited at his memorial service.)

During World War II the hotel was commandeered by the U.S. government and used to house Navy officers and their families. After the war it reopened as a hotel; but once again, in 1962, during the Cuban missile crisis, it was taken over and transformed into billets, this time for Army missile battalion troops. By then the jewel in Flagler's crown was a bit tarnished. When the crisis subsided and the Army pulled out, the hotel was in such a state of disrepair that only the Birdcage Lounge and the dance patio remained open. In the late 1960s the Peace Corps, wanting to accustom its volunteers to the conditions that they might find in developing countries, used part of the hotel for a training center.

In 1976 the Casa Marina was purchased and renovated by the Marriott Corporation, which has since sold it to the

Wyndham Corporation. Frost and Stevens are long gone, so we'll never know what they think of the Marriott/Wyndham makeover. Would they echo the sentiments of this contemporary writer?

Thorn parked . . . across the street from the Casa Marina Hotel. It was a palatial Mediterranean structure. . . . The Marriott people had decided the thick stucco walls of Flagler's old beauty should be replastered and dabbed with hipper colors, fitted out with flimsy brass lamps and cutely painted Mexican tile . . . until by now every vestige of the graceful original had been concealed by a series of slapdash contractors.

—James W. Hall, *Red Sky at Night*

Flagler Avenue

In the dark and cold of the morning they drove out the country road through the mist that hung heavy over the flat.

— Ernest Hemingway, *To Have and Have Not*

Flagler Avenue begins off Reynolds, across from the Casa Marina Hotel, and runs four miles southeast to the end of the key. Before it was renamed in honor of Henry Morrison Flagler, it was simply called Old County Road, presumably because it ran the length of the island, well outside Key West's corporate limits until 1889. (In May of that year, the Florida Legislature granted a new city charter that extended the city's boundaries to encompass the whole island.)

Biographers struggle to encapsulate the long life, vision, drive, and accomplishments of Flagler in one volume. To attempt to capture the essence of this man in a few paragraphs would be folly. Thus, for simplicity's sake, we'll divide his life

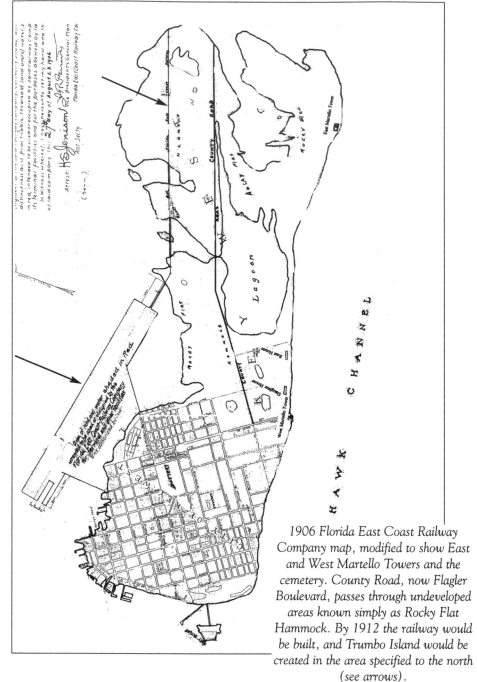

1906 Florida East Coast Railway Company map, modified to show East and West Martello Towers and the cemetery. County Road, now Flagler Boulevard, passes through undeveloped areas known simply as Rocky Flat Hammock. By 1912 the railway would be built, and Trumbo Island would be created in the area specified to the north (see arrows).

into two parts: the northern businessman who made a fortune and the master promoter who invested millions in developing Florida's east coast.

Born of humble origins in 1830, Flagler and his family moved from upstate New York to Ohio when he was seven. Throughout his early years and into his teens, Flagler exhibited a keen mind and natural bent for business. He married young; he and his wife, Mary, had five children in the 1850s, only one of whom survived to adulthood. After a series of struggles, successes, and failures, Flagler went into partnership with John D. Rockefeller, becoming his closest confidante and most trusted adviser. Together they propelled Standard Oil to dominance in the industry and earned fortunes for themselves.

In 1883 Flagler visited Florida for the first time. Even while he was on holiday, business was not far from his mind. He immediately recognized the need for improved transportation and better hotel accommodations, and apparently he had a vision of what was possible. By 1886 he began construction on what was to become the Renaissance-style Ponce de Leon Hotel in St. Augustine. To draw customers from Jacksonville and points north to this resort, Flagler purchased the Jacksonville, St. Augustine & Halifax River Railroad, improved it, and offered more attractive service and schedules. In the railroad business now, Flagler bought up shorter lines and cobbled together a railway company that was inching toward the tip of the peninsula.

By 1890 he had reached Daytona, where he purchased the Ormond Hotel. Until then Flagler had not built any railroad; he had merely purchased existing lines that could serve as feeders to his hotels. Bolstered by the success of his other transportation endeavors (primarily road-to-steamer), however, Flagler obtained a state charter authorizing him to build a railroad all the way to Miami. By the mid-1890s, he had pushed past the Indian River area and on into Palm Beach, where he built the world's largest resort hotel, the Royal Poinciana. A few years later, he constructed his second Palm Beach hotel, the Breakers.

In September 1895 Flagler's amalgamation of rail lines was renamed to reflect its broader reach: it became the Florida East Coast Railway, and the push farther south intensified.

When train service to Miami began on April 15, 1896, Miami was still a village, most accessible by boat from Key West, the largest city in Florida. This was to change. Soon after Miami incorporated in 1896, Flagler began donating land for municipal buildings and schools; he financed new streets and sidewalks; and he underwrote other municipal improvements. Due in part to Flagler's civic contributions, by 1902 Miami had grown from a small village to a burgeoning town of five thousand.

Flagler was not content to stop at Miami. Driven by a vision of an overseas railroad penetrating the Caribbean market (rail to Key West and steamer beyond), in 1905 Flagler announced that he would extend the Florida East Coast Railway all the way to Key West. To some it was "Flagler's Folly," but by 1912 the engineering marvel was being called the "Eighth Wonder of the World."

On January 22, 1912, Henry M. Flagler, nearly blind but his vision of the future intact, arrived aboard the first train to Key West. He and his wife disembarked at Trumbo Point, where they were greeted by Mayor J. N. Fogarty, marching bands, chorusing school girls, and a crowd of ten thousand.

Flagler Avenue and its predecessor, Old County Road, is home to one of the more macabre and also one of the more heinous Key West tales.

In the 1930s German immigrant "Count" Karl von Cosel, an X-ray technician at the Marine Hospital, became infatuated with a young tubercular patient, Elena Hoyos Mesa. After her death his infatuation intensified so much that he snatched her body from City Cemetery and took up housekeeping with the corpse in his home on Flagler Avenue. His secret love was discovered some seven years later, just long enough for him to escape prosecution because the statute of limitations had expired.

Our second tale smacks not of misguided love, but of unbridled hate. Islander Manuel Cabeza was living with a mulatto woman. Their relationship did not meet with the approval of the local Ku Klux Klan, which set about tarring and feathering him. Cabeza unveiled three of his assailants, located one of them later, and shot him to death. To escape mob justice he barricaded himself atop a building until the authorities could come and take him to jail. But mob rule prevailed anyway. Cabeza was removed from jail by Klansmen, beaten, and dragged behind a car down Old County Road, where he was hanged.

. . . thus veiling the greatest sight the town had seen since the Isleno had been lynched, years before, out on County Road and then hung up to swing from a telephone pole in the lights of all the cars that had come out to see it.

—Ernest Hemingway, *To Have and Have Not*

Trumbo Point

We could see the car ferries lying at the Trumbo dock where they would go around to head up for Garrison Bight.
>   —Ernest Hemingway, *To Have and Have Not*

Mile by mile Flagler's crews cleared a right-of-way, built up road bed, and laid track; span by span they bridged the gaps between the Keys. As they inched their way closer to Key West, one of the engineers realized an oversight.

Originally Key West was much smaller than it is today. There was simply not enough available land on that last key to build a terminal, especially not one large enough to accommodate Flagler's vision. No whistle stop here: the terminus at Key West would be a jumping-off point for travel onward to Cuba and other Caribbean destinations and a vast entrepôt for goods arriving, possibly even from the Pacific once the Panama Canal was completed.

When informed of the problem, Flagler cut right to the chase. "Then build some," he instructed.

In 1911 Joseph R. Parrot, Flagler's righthand man, stopped laying track, moved to the end of the line, and directed his attention toward the construction of a terminal and seaport. Of course, before he could build he needed land to build upon. Parrot summoned Howard Trumbo, the project engineer for the Overseas Railroad, and directed that dredge-and-fill operations begin.

Work went on around the clock. Soon two manmade peninsulas, Trumbo Island and Hilton Haven, were surrounding Garrison Bight. A drawbridge connected them. By the time Flagler and his wife arrived on that first train in 1912, Key West was larger by a hundred and thirty-four acres and the last train stop was indeed a gateway to the world. The seaport came complete with a seventeen-hundred-foot-long dock to which steamships could moor and on which their passengers could embark and disembark.

After seven years, at a cost of over seven hundred lives and some fifty million dollars, one could travel from New York City and other points north down to Miami and then onward to Key West. Flagler would die a year later and thus never see what became of his vision. In many ways it did manifest itself. There was regular passenger service to Havana, and goods from the Caribbean were transshipped from Key West. (For example, molasses imported from Cuba was stored in large tanks on the Florida East Coast Railway docks while awaiting shipment north by tank car.) But, subject to the vagaries of the international market, the enterprise was not the bonanza that Flagler had envisioned. In 1935 the dream ended when that killer hurricane struck. The foundation had, however, been laid for another dream. The automobile was now King of the Road: within years the Overseas Railroad was transformed into the Overseas Highway.

Trumbo Island eventually came to be called Trumbo Point. In 1917 construction began, and by February 1918 the Point had been transformed into a naval air station that served as a seaplane base and an aviation training center during World War I. In 1920 the Navy closed the air station. A couple of decades later, with threat of another world war looming, it was reopened.

By the early 1940s, World War II was raging, and we were now in it. Our Navy needed a place to expand its operations. It took over the old railroad yards and seaport, and turned the entire point into the Navy base that it is today.

The Aviators

Trumbo Point is an area into which most of us do not venture. Indeed, access to the naval base there is restricted to military personnel and their dependents. Thus, the following chapter is a rendering of sheer bookwork; the streets the same to you as me: lines delineated on an unexplored portion of a map.

Chuck turned on Palm Avenue and drove across the arching Garrison Bight bridge, past the naval base. Palm became Eaton as he headed into Old Town.

—Stuart Woods, *Choke*

Whiting and Mustin Streets
The streets on the Point are named for U.S. Navy aviation pioneers. We group Whiting and Mustin together not because one runs off the other, but because both aviators for whom the

streets are named graduated from the first U.S. Navy Aviation Training Course in 1915. They may not, however, have started together.

In 1914 the abandoned Navy Yard in Pensacola, Florida, was turned into a training station for fledgling aviators, and the first class was enrolled. It is not clear if Kenneth Whiting and Henry C. Mustin were classmates in that first class, the second class, or were in separate classes, but within a year Mustin would make aviation history. He became the first pilot to take off from a ship at sea. He accomplished this by catapulting off the stern of the U.S.S. *North Carolina* in Pensacola Bay.

Whiting would go on to become the commander of the American naval air units in France during World War I. In his honor, Whiting Field, located in the Florida Panhandle near Pensacola, was commissioned in July 1943. Graduating some seven hundred fixed-wing pilots and four hundred and seventy-five helicopter pilots annually, it is our military's primary base for Navy and Marine Corps flight training.

Ely Street

Ely Street runs off Palm, but is blocked to civilian traffic by a guard house. The street is named after Eugene Ely.

Ely, by all accounts an intrepid flyer (rain, shine, fog, or sleet), was the first person to land an airplane on a ship at sea. On January 18, 1916, he landed his Curtiss aero plane on the warship *Pennsylvania*.

The Aviators

Chambers Street
*. . . he rounded the island to Chambers Street where he could see
. . .Miranda sitting on one of the guides' lockers at the dock.*
—Thomas McGuane, *Ninety-Two in the Shade*

Lieutenant Reed M. Chambers teamed up with aviation ace Eddie Rickenbacker to make more military aviation history. While assigned to the 94th Aero Squadron in France, they flew the first American combat air patrol on April 14, 1918.

Soon after the Armistice, both discharged now, the two men teamed up again. Rickenbacker, a national hero (twenty-six aces and a Congressional Medal of Honor) turned down lucrative offers from Hollywood and the advertising industry in order to continue pursuing his passion. He and Chambers went into the aerial mapping business on the West Coast. In the mid-1920s Chambers moved to Florida, where he organized Florida Airways. In 1928 he founded the U.S. Aircraft Insurance Group.

Halsey Street
William Frederick Halsey Jr., the son of a Navy officer, continued his family's tradition. Educated at the Naval Academy at Annapolis, he distinguished himself (Navy Cross) as a destroyer commander in World War I. At an age when most of us are firmly set in our ways, the fifty-two-year-old Halsey made a career adjustment: he became a naval aviator and distinguished himself even more in the next war. As vice-admiral in command of a Pacific carrier division, he directed air raids on the Gilbert, Marshall, Wake, and Marcus Islands. Two years later he was promoted to admiral and given command of all Southwest

Asia naval forces. He mopped up that part of the Pacific and was then awarded command of the Third Fleet, which worked with the Fifth to help bring Japan to its knees.

General Douglas MacArthur considered Halsey to be the greatest fighting admiral of World War II, and Hollywood capitalized on his fame. In 1960 *The Gallant Hours* starred James Cagney as "Bull" Halsey, Dennis Weaver as Lieutenant Commander Andy Lowe, and highlighed the gallantry and daring of both men.

Mitscher and Flagg Avenues

Halsey and Mitscher Avenues run roughly parallel to each other and are connected by Flagg Street at their western ends. Like Stickney, there are two motorways bearing the name Flagg. Both are named after Captain Allan P. Flagg, the commanding officer of the Naval Air Station from 1941 to 1945.

During that same period, Admiral Marc Andrew Mitscher was twelve time zones away from Key West. His last assignment of the war was to command Task Force 58, a force of swift aircraft carriers, cruisers, battleships, and destroyers that pushed the Japanese military from the Marshall Islands westward to their home bases.

Like Halsey, Mitscher was an Annapolis graduate; unlike Halsey, he learned to fly while still a young officer. In 1915, soon after leaving the Naval Academy, he attended flight school in Pensacola. Mitscher, probably in the class after Mustin and Whiting, is ranked as the thirty-second Navy officer to earn his wings.

Between the wars Mitscher honed his skills aboard aircraft

tenders and carriers, earning a berth as the executive officer of the *Saratoga*, the Navy's first real aircraft carrier. Early in the Second World War, Mitscher was in command of a new carrier, the *Hornet*, from which the first air raids over Japan were launched. But it was in the end game that Mitscher really stood out (three Distinguished Service Medals). Starting on the Marshall Islands, where his air forces provided cover for the American amphibious landing on heavily defended Kwajalein, Mitscher's Task Force 58 pounded the Japanese off the Caroline and Palau Islands, the Marianas, and other Nipponese strongholds in the Western Pacific.

After the war Mitscher's distinguished service was recognized. He was appointed deputy chief of naval operations, then made full admiral and given command of the Atlantic-based Eighth Fleet. He would not serve long, however. In 1947, at the age of sixty, Mitscher died.

Eastern Half of Key West

At this point we've covered roughly half the island (thanks to landfill, an area larger than the original Key West itself), and we've still got another half to go. Yet, as you can see, there are not that many pages left.

Much of the eastern half of Key West is undeveloped or contains development that is not residential. The Salt Ponds are here, as are the airport and its runway. And beyond the airstrip are U.S. government and other public properties on either side of Government Road. Somewhere in this area, perhaps where so many tourists deplane and see Key West for the first time, is where, centuries ago, the Spaniards explored, spotted all those bones, and gave the island its first name.

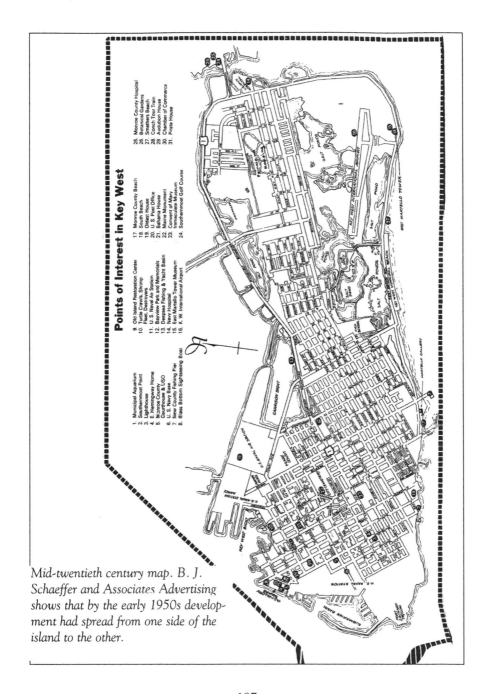

Points of Interest in Key West

1. Municipal Aquarium
2. Southernmost Point
3. Lighthouse
4. E. Hemingway Home
5. Monroe County Courthouse & USO
6. U. S. Navy Base
7. New County Fishing Pier
8. Glass Bottom Sightseeing Boat
9. Old Island Restoration Center
10. Turtle Crawls, Shrimp Fleet, Destroyers
11. U. S. Naval Air Station
12. Bayview Park and Memorials
13. Deepsea Fishing & Yacht Basin
14. New Hospital
15. East Martello Tower Museum
16. K. W. International Airport
17. Monroe County Beach
18. South Beach
19. Oldest House
20. U. S. Post Office
21. Bahama House
22. Maine Monument
23. Convent of Mary Immaculate Museum
24. Southernmost Golf Course
25. Monroe County Hospital
26. Botanical Gardens
27. Smathers Beach
28. Conch Tour Train
29. Audubon House
30. Chamber of Commerce
31. Pirate House

Mid-twentieth century map. B. J.
Schaeffer and Associates Advertising
shows that by the early 1950s development had spread from one side of the
island to the other.

Meacham Field

*The sun was still low in the sky when the Air Sunshine DC-3 glided
in over the salt pond and put down at Key West International
Airport.*

—Burt Hirschfeld, *Key West*

In March of 1926 a stranger rolled into Key West in search of a
deal. He had been heralded by an advance man of some
renown, W. C. Barron, founder of Barron's financial magazine.
Malcolm Meacham, a promoter whose associates had developed Palm Beach, had even grander ideas in mind for Key West.
All he needed was the land, and he got it. At $500 a pop, he
spent $500,000 for a thousand acres of land cobbled together by
Key West Realty Company from various interests of salt producers. Though he had big plans that would have meant filling
the Salt Ponds had he obtained even more land, he started
small and on firmer ground. He sold subdivided lots along Old
County Road (today's Flagler Avenue), and he leased land to a
fledgling airline.

In September 1927 Pan American Airways leased twenty-
five acres from Meacham, built an "airdrome" (marl airstrip and
small hangar), and called it Meacham Field. Within months
the airline was flying international mail from Key West to
Havana. By January 1928 Pan Am had initiated regular passenger service to Cuba. On the first flights, humans were not the
only passengers; homing pigeons were also aboard. In case of
emergency over water they were to be released carrying an SOS
back to Pan Am's home office, Pigeon House Patio, on
Whitehead.

As for Meacham, his dreams crashed with the stock market

in 1929, and his vast holdings reverted back to Key West Realty. Much of it has since remained in its natural state.

Pan Am closed its Key West shop in 1939, but the airfield continued to operate. On July 4, 1957, Congressman Dante Fascell dedicated Key West International Airport at Meacham Field. By then the wooden shanties that served Pan Am had been demolished, the land cleared, and a spanking new terminal built. It still stands today, adding a funky touch to the rapidly gentrifying island.

Access to the airport is via Feraldo Circle off South Roosevelt. The circle is named for George Feraldo, a local stunt and acrobatic pilot.

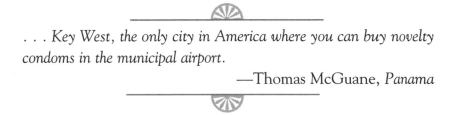

. . . Key West, the only city in America where you can buy novelty condoms in the municipal airport.

—Thomas McGuane, *Panama*

A couple of miles from the airport, on the other side of the westernmost Salt Ponds, is a quiet residential neighborhood. Here we have more mysterious ladies: Bertha, Blanche, and Josephine, streets whose names are of unknown origin.

Dennis and Duncombe Streets

At the high school he cut onto Bertha Street and then Roosevelt Boulevard toward the airport, as if on his way to catch a plane.

—Burt Hirschfeld, *Key West*

Dennis Street runs off Flagler Avenue and dead ends a few blocks later on what used to be salt flats. It is named in honor of William C. Dennis, a refined and wealthy islander who was in favor of Florida's secession from the Union. Most probably, however, the street bears his name not for his Southern sympathies, but for his cultivation of the Salt Ponds. In 1851 Dennis purchased half of Charles Howe's controlling interest in the dominant salt company on the island and undertook its management. He manufactured salt and ran the company until he died in 1864.

Duncombe Street, parallel to Dennis, also runs off Flagler, but just for a block. It is named for William Duncombe Cash, a transplanted Bahamian who made good in his new hometown. Like Dennis, he was a businessman. W. D. Cash's Groceries, Provisions and Ship Chandlery was located at the corner of Duval and Front Streets. Also like Dennis, Cash was a Southern sympathizer. During the Civil War he was arrested on charges of making "treasonable utterances" (according to Browne) and confined to Ft. Taylor for a few weeks before negotiating his release by signing a *parole d'honeur*. Apparently his support of the Confederate cause did not hurt him locally. He was elected mayor and then chosen to be the first president of the Key West Chamber of Commerce, where he served from 1902 to 1910.

As a businessman, Cash also got involved in the salt manufacturing industry when he bought the salt-work interests of C. Howe and E. Howe, who were probably offspring of Charles Howe. In 1906 the Key West Realty Company purchased Cash's holdings and divided the dry land into town lots. Given its location, Duncombe Street is probably so named because of the mayor's venture into the salt business.

Key West High School is set back **off Duncombe Street,** some of it on land that was part of the salt works and had to be filled before the school could be built. For years salt pans could still be seen on campus.

Across from the Salt Ponds that extend beyond the campus, between Government Road and Flagler Avenue, is a long, linear neighborhood that stretches two miles along Riviera Canal. The canal, dug in the 1930s, exits the island beneath North Roosevelt Boulevard. In its original state, before the northern edges of the island were filled, a channel allowed tidal flow from the Gulf to the Salt Ponds.

Riviera Drive is a mix of luxury homes, cement-block Florida specials, and dumps disguised by vegetation. Monty stopped . . . on Riviera. The wind had gone still and smells of salt rot from the canal wafted out to the road.

—Tom Corcoran, *Octopus Alibi*

A couple of the street names, Venetian and Riviera, reflect their proximity to the canal. Others were named for water-locked Caribbean countries: Bahama, Jamaica, and Trinidad Drives.

The rest, Airport Boulevard and Sunrise Drive and Sunrise Lane, are named for obvious reasons. In 1998 there were a couple of houses up for sale at 3628 Sunrise Drive. On the canal, 5 bedrooms, 5 baths, combined area of 3,000 sq. ft., the asking price a cool $1.5 million. Not bad for a guy who got his start living in a seedy walk-up over on Waddell. The newspaper article said that the owner was looking for a smaller place in the area. One wonders, though. Perhaps Margaritaville was simply closing in on Jimmy Buffett.

. . . a boatload of Cuban refugees had found its way into the canal. Sunburned, destitute, they appealed to a resident for help. They had no way to know that their benefactor, the man who had given them Cokes and snacks . . . was Jimmy Buffett.

—Tom Corcoran, *Octopus Alibi*

George to Twentieth Streets

"Go right!" he said at the intersection with Duck Avenue. She turned and proceeded along. . . . They went by an empty ballpark approaching Kennedy Drive where they would have to make a turn.
— John Leslie, *Damaged Goods*

The north side of Flagler Boulevard contains the most newly developed part of Key West. As late as 1942, the only infrastructure in much of this area was Flagler and the numerically marked streets that ran off it. During the war, however, development was spurred by the construction of military housing; within a decade, suburbia was firmly entrenched in this sector of the key.

As you may have noticed, the street names have been accruing in roughly chronological order as development marches across the island. That is, we had streets named for

Simonton, Whitehead, and other pioneers back in Old Town, and, most recently, Duncombe Street (near the salt flats) named after a prominent turn-of-the-century islander. This pattern continues.

As more development engulfed the rest of the island, however, some of the street names began to sound like they could be anywhere. Starting with First Street, there is a string of numerically ordered streets that run to Twentieth. But, as we will see, this monotony is broken by Kennedy Drive, Macmillan Street, and Boog Powell Court.

Patterson Avenue

Patterson Avenue runs off George, angles a bit at Sixth, and then jumps the City Boat Basin to end at Twelfth Street.

Alexander Patterson came to Key West early enough to be an inaugural member of St. Paul's Episcopal Church in 1832. By mid-decade he was one of the island's principal merchants. His store was located near the harbor, at the foot of Whitehead, where it served his other interests well. As a sideline, Patterson was an auctioneer for the goods salvaged from the reef wrecks. A prominent citizen, between 1845 and 1868 Patterson served as mayor of Key West for four terms of varying length.

Patterson and his helpmeet, described as a good woman of Christian virtue and great charity, had two sons and four daughters. Most probably, Patterson Avenue is named for number one son, George Browne Patterson.

George married well and wisely (the daughter of Judge Winer Bethel), and went on to establish himself as an island politico. Twice, in 1876 and again in 1890, he served as U.S. district attorney. Patterson was so well regarded by his

Republican Party that they nominated him to run for Congress in 1900. His Key West home, a Queen Anne replica built after the devastating 1886 fire, can be seen at **522 Caroline**.

Fogarty Street

Fogarty Street is named for the man who greeted Henry Flagler and wife when they got off the train at the end of its maiden run to Key West. Mayor Joseph N. Fogarty was elected to office in 1905 and served a number of terms that stretched into the mid-1910s.

During his tenure, Fogarty had to deal with a moral minority that looked askance at drinking on the bawdy island. Twenty-five percent of the voters signed a petition to put the issue of abolition of saloons on the 1907 ballot. At stake were thirty-eight licensed saloons, the livelihood of their proprietors, and the spirits of their customers. Fogarty, true Irishman that he was, sided with the "wets," who won by a slim margin and thus maintained the island tradition that is so evident today.

Fogarty was also involved in charitable causes. A medical doctor by profession, Dr. Fogarty helped establish the *Casa del Pobre* (Mercedes Hospital) in the old Gato Mansion at the corner of Division (Truman) and Salt Pond Road (now Jose Marti Boulevard). He then contributed generously to maintain it, donated medical instruments and equipment, served as hospital director, and volunteered his services once a month.

Gogarty of Fogarty

Irish poet Oliver St. John Gogarty, good friend of novelist James Joyce, once lived at First and Fogarty. One of his earlier domiciles was a Martello tower on the Irish coast that he shared with Joyce. Apparently Joyce incorporated their experience in one of his most difficult novels. Main character Stephen Dedalus and his bud, Bucky Milligan, also turned a tower into their home in *Ulysses*.

Harris Avenue

It is difficult to tell which "Harris" Harris Avenue is named for. There is Dr. J. Vining Harris, a physician and wealthy Key Wester who owned almost all of Sugar Loaf Key, on which he experimented with the cultivation of sponges. And there is Jeptha Vining Harris, a prominent island lawyer and criminal court judge who appears to be the son of Dr. Harris. Finally, there is the Honorable W. Hunt Harris, a prominent politician who was president of the Florida Senate from 1907 to 1909. Any one of these men could be the claimant.

If flair and vivacity were the criteria for selection, my nod would go to Jephtha (1865–1936). By taking William Curry's youngest daughter as his bride, he married into one of the wealthiest families in Florida, and her dowry must have been considerable. The Harrises built and resided in a Queen Anne mansion at the corner of Duval and South Streets, the "Southernmost House" in the United States (until Ms. Strabel built her more modest abode around the corner).

Seidenberg Avenue

Seidenberg Avenue is named in honor of cigar manufacturer William Seidenberg.

During the 1800s cigar smoking in America was as common as cigarette smoking had been in the 1900s until the surgeon general informed us of its hazard to our health. In the

1850s the U.S. government capitalized on this popularity by levying a hefty tax on imported cigars. Seidenberg also capitalized. Inasmuch as the tariff applied to rolled cigars only, he purchased a tobacco plantation in Cuba, established himself in Key West, and imported the leaf from his plantation, thus becoming a pioneer in corporate vertical integration.

One of the big three producers on the island, Seidenberg and Company owned *La Rosa Espaniola*, which employed some six hundred hands at its height of production. Continually beset by problems, Seidenberg was constantly struggling. In the early 1880s his severe financial problems caused his underwriter, Charles T. Merrill, to go under, never to surface again as a banker. Seidenberg, however, did recover and was doing well when the great fire of 1886 destroyed his factory and that of his major competitor, Vicente Ybor. Ybor relocated to Tampa. Seidenberg stuck it out and rebuilt immediately, a decision he would come to regret within years.

By 1894 labor troubles were rearing their contentious heads at *La Rosa Espaniola*. Daily meetings of management with the board of trade were commonplace, investigations the norm. To solve his problem Seidenberg decided to do away with its source. He would no longer employ Cubans and would start hiring Spaniards to fill their slots. Besides the financial hardship this would cause his furloughed employees, the Cuban community was also concerned that Seidenberg's solution would result in a "fifth column" in their midst.

As noted earlier, Key West was a hotbed of Cuban revolutionary fervor in the 1890s. If Seidenberg's scheme worked out, hundreds of Spaniards, some of them perhaps Spanish government operatives, would be living cheek-by-jowl with Cubans on the small island. Secrecy would be difficult. So, Seidenberg had run afoul of both labor and political sentiment, and when the lawyers got involved, matters went from bad to their complicated worst.

Cuban patriots rallied by hiring a lawyer, Horatio Rubens, who charged U.S. government officials (Browne, the collector of customs; Patterson, the district attorney we just met; and Bethel, immigration inspector) with abetting a violation of U.S. contract labor laws. The case went to Washington, where the secretaries of state and treasury, as well as the attorney general, got involved. Patterson et al. were cleared, but Seidenberg was charged with violating alien contract law and faced imminent arrest. Eventually the case was settled in U.S. District Court in Louisiana, and the charges were dropped. By then Seidenberg had had enough. He pulled up stakes and joined Ybor in Tampa.

Running parallel to Seidenberg is Staples Avenue. The origin of this street name is unknown. There is, however, a link to the cigar industry here. On Third Street, between Staples and Flagler, a large, four-story factory, pride of the Havana-American Cigar Company, dominated the empty spaces on the outskirts of town for decades.

Macmillan Street and Kennedy Drive

Originally Fifth Street, Macmillan Street cuts through Patterson, Fogarty, and Harris before turning back into Fifth. Fifth became Macmillan in honor of former British Prime Minister Harold Macmillan. But why? Why would the city fathers in Key West name one of their streets for a member of the book-publishing family who became British prime minister, served for years, and then had to resign in the face of scandal?

In the spring of 1961, a few months after assuming office, President John Fitzgerald Kennedy had met with Prime Minister Macmillan on the island. Ostensibly convened to discuss the crisis in Laos, their meeting was probably a prelude to the Bay of Pigs invasion that followed three weeks after the mini-summit. Years later Fifth Street was renamed in commemoration of his visit.

A year before he was assassinated, Kennedy made a second visit to Key West. In November of 1962, weeks after the Cuban missile crisis had been resolved, Kennedy returned to the island. This visit was more celebratory than his first: he came to express his gratitude to the various armed forces for the role they played in averting a nuclear conflagration. It was a day trip: after flying into Boca Chica Naval Air Station, he took a two-hour whirlwind tour of the area. Reportedly, his motorcade zoomed about town, swerving to avoid excited dogs. The president, seated comfortably in his open convertible, could be seen by all.

They went by an empty ballpark approaching Kennedy Drive where they would have to make a turn. If they turned right they'd be back on Roosevelt Boulevard.

—John Leslie, *Damaged Goods*

Kennedy Drive, formerly Thirteenth Street, is a busy thoroughfare. It connects Flagler and North Roosevelt, and forms the western boundary of the **Key West High School sports**

complex. A couple of "streets" named for major league baseball players run off Kennedy. Albury Avenue, really an entrance to part of the complex, is named for Key Wester Vic Albury, who pitched for the Minnesota Twins; Boog Powell Court, running off Glynn Archer Jr. Street, was named for another islander who probably faced Albury when he was on the mound.

Boog Powell Court

John "Boog" Powell was a graduate of Key West High and a "Fighting Conch" who used his athletic ability to earn a livelihood and a modicum of fame. After putting in some journeyman years in the Baltimore Orioles' farm system, Boog was called up to the parent club. There he continued to develop. In 1969 the power-hitting first baseman's 37 home runs and 121 RBI's propelled the Orioles into the World Series, where they lost to those amazing New York Mets (who overcame 200-1 odds to win the championship).

Nineteen-seventy was another stellar season for Powell. He was voted the American League's Most Valuable Player, and the Orioles won the World Series. During his career, which he ended in 1972, the power hitter batted .266 and hit 339 home runs.

Glynn Archer Jr. Street

Glynn Archer Jr. Street, a block east of Kennedy, forms the eastern boundary of the sports complex. Like Kennedy, it links Flagler and Roosevelt, and was formerly a numerically designated street (Fourteenth).

The Archers have left their mark on Key West education.

Glynn Archer Sr. was an educator who served as chairman of the board of education for a number of years. His son, Glynn Archer Jr., did not fall far from the tree. A graduate of Key West High School (when it was still located on White Street), Archer eventually became principal of his alma mater. Then, in 1972, he became assistant superintendent of schools for Monroe County. Archer died in 1996.

When they built a shopping center over an old salt marsh, the sea birds sometimes circle the same place for a year or more, coming back to check daily to see if there isn't some little chance those department stores and pharmacies and cinemas won't go as quickly as they'd come.

—Thomas McGuane, *Panama*

Searstown, located inland **off North Roosevelt**, is not named in tribute to Sears School, the island's first free school. More prosaically, it was named for the leading retailer, Sears, Roebuck and Company, which anchors Key West's largest shopping center. As indicated by McGuane, Searstown was built on landfill. Most of the land along the Gulf between Kennedy and the Navy Hospital at the northeastern end of the key is the product of dredge and fill.

Toppino Avenue, running a long block to connect North Roosevelt to inland residential neighborhoods, is named for another master tamer of the environment, Charles Toppino. Toppino and Sons Construction is in the concrete-manufacturing business. It poured the concrete for the bridges and paved the way from the mainland to mile zero.

Farther inland, **between Donald and Duck Avenues**, is the housing development that spurred eastward development. Built by the U.S. Navy, **Poinciana Housing** is a tangle of streets, courts, and cul-de-sacs, all named for Navy men and officers. No longer a haven for Navy dependents, it now serves as a low-income housing project.

Dunlap Drive, which snakes from Duck to Nineteenth Street, is named for Robert Dunlap, a Marine who was awarded the Congressional Medal of Honor. **Hoey Road** is named after Captain Granville Hoey, the commanding officer (CO) of the Naval Air Station (NAS) before World War II. **Truesdell Court** honors the memory of Captain W. H. Truesdell, CO of the Key West Fleet Sonar School. **Spaulding Court** is named for Lieutenant Ralph Spaulding, a Navy medical officer. **Flagg Court**, as mentioned in the section on Trumbo Point, is named after Captain Allan P. Flagg, CO of NAS from 1943 to 1945. **Reordan Court** bears the name of another CO, Captain Charles E. Reordan, and **Scholtz Court** honors Commander David Scholtz. Ellsburg, for whom **Ellsburg Court** is named, was probably either a Navy submariner or a salvage diver. Finally, **Morgan Court** is named after World War II gunner Charles Morgan, and **Brunson Court** for Admiral Brunson.

Pearlman Court

When you look at a Key West map, the area bounded by Northside and Donald, and Sixteenth to Eighteenth Terrace appears to be a tilted grid. In fact, it is the rest of the island that is out of sync with the compass. Pearlman Terrace and Pearlman Court are the only two streets in Key West that run true east-west. These and the streets just specified are the only ones on the island that are aligned with true north. The rest of the key's grid system originated from the harbor, which faces northwest. Consequently, Key West's streets run northwest-southeast and southwest-northeast.

The area around Pearlman Terrace and Court was originally called Pearlman Estates. Joe Pearlman was born in Romania in 1892. His family immigrated to Key West in 1904, where he was quite successful in two very diverse businesses: retail and construction. Pearlman's Quality Store was a mainstay on Duval for almost four decades. His construction enterprises, the Monroe Land Development Company and CBS Construction Company, built much of the islands' Navy housing during World War II; afterward he expanded into building concrete-block, single-family civilian homes. Pearlman was a civic leader and important member of Key West's Jewish community. He and his wife had three children, Donald, Paula, and Cindy. Their names can be found on avenues in this residential neighborhood.

The place was identical to all the other cement-block homes that were built north of Atlantic and west of Bertha in the late 1960s. Most had carports and basic trimmed shrubs. . . .

—Tom Corcoran, *The Mango Opera*

Roosevelt Boulevard

*Most new arrivals come by car across the Overseas Highway—
Route 1—from the mainland. He went to where the Honda was
parked and drove onto Roosevelt Boulevard past the Naval Hospital
past the Key Wester.*

—Burt Hirschfeld, *Key West*

Roosevelt Boulevard, North and
South, mark the end of our tour. Originating where U.S. 1
crosses the Cow Key Channel and enters Key West, North
Roosevelt veers right and hugs the Gulf for a couple of miles
before turning into Truman. Turning left at the same junction
is Highway A1A, which instantly turns into South Roosevelt as
it wraps around the eastern end of the key, passes the East
Martello Tower, and then borders Hawk Channel, beyond
which lie the Straits of Florida.

Almost ten miles long (from where North Roosevelt turns

into Truman in the old North Beach area to where South Roosevelt ends at Bertha Street), Roosevelt wraps around the island to become its longest road.

The boulevard is named for our longest-serving president, Franklin Delano Roosevelt. During his administration Key West underwent some very necessary formative changes. By 1934 Florida's most affluent city had turned into one of its most impoverished, and it was so riddled with debt that it surrendered its governance to the State of Florida.

Governor David Sholtz, in turn, looked to the federal government for assistance. Under the guidance of young Julius Stone Jr. (thirty-three years old and armed with a Harvard Ph.D. in organic chemistry), the Federal Emergency Relief Administration set about rehabilitating the economy of the island. Some four thousand Key Westers volunteered to clean up the shabby island; schools for fishing guides and motel maids were established; guest houses were renovated; and a yacht basin was created out of the abandoned submarine base. Within a year of his arrival, Stone began promoting the island as a premier destination for tourists, and they poured in. The revival was short-lived, however. In 1935 the massive Labor Day hurricane destroyed the railroad, thereby cutting Key West's economic lifeline to the mainland until the highway was completed a few years later.

On February 19, 1939, Roosevelt became the only U.S. president to drive the entire length of the Overseas Highway. By then the transition was complete. Starting from the edge of the harbor, Key West had been built facing its lifelink, the sea. Now most people and goods entered via U.S. 1 from the opposite end, and the island had, in effect, been turned into a peninsula.

The Streets of Key West

From Miami to Key West on the Overseas Highway. Two lanes, hopping from key to key past diners closed for the night, past marinas . . . and grubby motels used only by day fishermen or couples in a hurry.

—Burt Hirschfeld, *Key West*

Smathers Beach

Joey picked his way through the traffic on A1A, slipped through the ranks of bicycles and scooters streaming along the broad promenade that flanked the road, found a gap between the joggers, and stepped onto Smathers Beach.

—Laurence Shames, *Florida Straits*

George Armistead Smathers hails from a family whose roots are in New Jersey, but whose branches have reached out into Florida and its politics. Born in Atlantic City in 1913, young George moved to Miami when he was six and stayed on to attain all of his formal education in Florida. A lawyer by profession (University of Florida Law School, 1938), Smathers began in private practice and then served as an assistant district attorney before joining the Marines during World War II. After the war he went into politics, where he won every race he ran. He served two terms in the U.S. House of Representatives (1947–1951) and three in the Senate (1951–1969). Smathers' first run for the Senate was the most memorable. During a vitriolic campaign at the height of the Cold War, he unseated long-serving Claude Pepper by tagging the liberal senator with the pejoration, "Red Pepper." After his public service, Smathers returned to private practice in Washington and Miami.

On a different note, but one of probably much more interest in laid-back Key West, songwriter and singer Jimmy Buffet unveiled his second live album at a Smathers Beach party on October 27, 1990. *Feeding Frenzy* had been recorded while the balladeer was on tour during the summer, but held for a release that would correspond with the island's Fantasy Fest celebration in the fall.

An odd beach Smathers was, not like Jones Beach, Rockaway, or Coney Island. It was made of old coral, the bigger pieces resembling knucklebones, the smaller ones looking like shards and ribs from a well-picked chicken. Over the coral was a layer of imported sand.
　　　　　　　　　　　　　　—Laurence Shames, *Florida Straits*

Houseboat Row

. . . and drove out along Roosevelt Boulevard to where a line of houseboats were moored in Cow Key Channel.

—Burt Hirschfeld, *Key West*

our miles and almost two centuries removed from where we started, we are now at the eastern edge of the island. Had we been here just a few years ago, we would have found a seaside community that was struggling to hang on. The twenty-six houseboats that made up the row, floating homes that added to the funky charm of the island, were in jeopardy—and not just from hurricanes like Georges that battered the key in the summer of 1998.

Apparently one islander's funk is another's eyesore, and some Key Westers wanted the community that had been at

Houseboat Row

Houseboat Row, no longer a landmark.

Now just another esplanade.

water's edge since the Fifties relegated to the history books. They got their way. Now that mix of hovel, kitsch, and elegance is gone. The concrete bulkhead is still there, but except for the remains of a few boats partially submerged in the shallows, one would never know that this area was once home to many people. All that remains is an esplanade that, one day, will probably play host to a historical marker that can be read by nearby residents and tourists.

Gloom shrouded Key West . . . as she turned onto South Roosevelt, passing the remains of Houseboat Row. . . .
—Dorothy Francis, *Conch Shell Murder*

Across Roosevelt, across from where the first of the house-boats was moored, is the **Double Tree Grand Key Resort**, a gargantuan hotel and condominium complex. Next to it, across from where the rest of the houseboats once floated, construction on an even grander scale was recently underway. By the time you read this, SaltPonds Condominiums, OceanWalk Apartment Homes, Seaside Residences, and the SunriseSuites Resort will probably be in place.

Que sera, sera.

No, the proposal that worried him was that island development near the top of Cow Key Channel.

—Tom Corcoran, *Octopus Alibi*

Hereafter

I pedaled by the cemetery. The gates were still open and I rode in, taking the familiar narrow paved paths with their street markers. . . . Gone for the most part are those gritty Conch faces . . . buried along with my parents and cousins in the concrete tombs stacked one on top of the other in the city cemetery.

—John Leslie, *Killing Me Softly*

We have gone from one end of the island to the other, naming the streets, identifying the origins of their names, outlining matters of historic interest along the way, and, to a much lesser extent, pointing out what might be of contemporary interest. There is only one part of the island that has been passed over.

I have mentioned the **City Cemetery** a number of times, and we have covered the streets skirting its periphery. But the streets within its boundary are unremarkable. The avenues run parallel and numerically, First through Eighth; four of the remaining streets are named for plants or trees; and the other two, Clara and Pauline, for unknown women. But many of its inhabitants are, by now, well known to us.

Ellen Mallory is here. She was laid to rest next to a couple of her grandchildren who died much too young. The wealthy, William Curry and William Von Phister, share ground with their more humble neighbors, like Abe Sawyer, Key West's most renowned midget. Mercedes Gato, for whom the *Casa del Pobre* was named, is here, buried in the Catholic section, but her wealthy husband, Eduardo, somehow ended up in native soil back in Cuba.

The **Catholic Cemetery**, which was added to the original 1847 cemetery in 1868, occupies ten thousand square yards inside the corner of Angela and Frances. The Toppino Family Mausoleum, no doubt made of concrete, is here, not far from the plot that holds pioneer priests from St. Mary's, Star of the Sea.

The smaller **Jewish Cemetery** occupies an opposite corner at Frances and Olivia. Here we find merchants Appelrouth and Aronovitz, and developer Joe Pearlman.

Outside the gate that reads "B'nai Zion," back toward the cemetery's Laurel "Street," is located the mausoleum that houses deceased members of the Dr. Felix Varela Lodge. One hopes that they have joined the good doctor, who may be destined for sainthood. Catherine Lowe, who had the audacity to flaunt her allegiance to the Confederacy, is not far away. And Dr. J. Y. Porter (1847–1927), who was born and died in the same room (but whose accomplishments in between were far-reaching),

The Jewish section.

Sloppy Joe's grave marker.

J.V. Harris's grave marker.

shares a multi-generational plot with wife Louisa, eldest of the Curry daughters, and their grandchild, Jessie Porter Newton.

Hemingway's buddies, Josie "Sloppy Joe" Russell and Charles Thompson, are here with their families. Judge J. Vining Harris, no longer able to claim the distinction of living in the "southernmost" house, has permanent residency. And Richard Peacon's digs may not be on par with his "Octagon House," but the upkeep is much less demanding.

Finally, two gentlemen, neither of whom has a street in Key West named in his honor, deserve our attention and gratitude. Entombed within a hundred feet of each other are Walter C. Maloney and Jefferson B. Browne. Maloney (1813–1884), who drew on Whitehead's writings to put together Key West's first history, presumably occupies the lowest tier in the stack of tombs that resembles a wedding cake. Browne (1857–1937), his eternal neighbor, was close in life as well. In writing his 1911 update, *Key West: The Old and the New*, Browne drew liberally on Maloney's *A Sketch of Key West*. In his will Judge Browne stipulated that his wine and liquor collection be divided equally among a coterie of designated friends. He then requested that they get together, pour out a libation, and, holding it aloft, say, "Here's to Jeff Browne."

I raise my pen. Let it be said, "Here's to Jeff Browne, Walt Maloney, and Will Whitehead."

References

Books

Browne, Jefferson B. *Key West: The Old and the New* (facsimile reproduction of 1912 edition). Gainesville, Florida: University of Florida Press, 1973.

Cox, Christopher. *A Key West Companion.* New York, New York: St. Martin's Press, 1983.

Kaufelt, Lynn Mitsuko. *Key West Writers and Their Houses.* Englewood, Florida: Pineapple Press and Omnigraphics, 1986.

Langley, Joan, and Wright Langley. *Key West: Images of the Past.* Key West, Florida: 1982.

Langley, Wright, and Stan Windhorn. *Yesterday's Key West.* Miami, Florida: Seeman Publishing, 1973.

Maloney, Walter C. *A Sketch of the History of Key West, Florida* (facsimile reproduction of 1876 edition). Gainesville, Florida: University of Florida Press, 1968.

McIver, Stuart B. *Hemingway's Key West*. Sarasota, Florida: Pineapple Press, 1993.

McLendon, James. *PAPA: Hemingway in Key West*. New York, New York: Popular Library, 1972.

Morris, Allen. *The Florida Handbook, 1971–1972*. Tallahassee, Florida: Peninsular Publishing, 1971.

Nichols, Stephen. *A Chronological History of Key West*. Key West, Florida: Key West Images of the Past, 1996.

Ogle, Maureen. *Key West: History of an Island of Dreams*. Gainesville, Florida: University Press of Florida, 2003.

Perez, Elizabeth. *Florida Cuban Heritage Trail*. Tallahassee, Florida: Florida Department of State, 1994.

Stevenson, George. *Stevenson's Key West Sketch Book and Guide*. Key West, Florida: G.B. Stevenson, 1957.

Viele, John. *The Florida Keys, A History of the Pioneers*. Sarasota, Florida: Pineapple Press, 1996.

Williams, Joy. *The Florida Keys, A History and Guide*. New York, NY: Random House, 1988.

Articles

Aitland, Patti. "Dr. J. Y. Porter," *Martello*, no. 2 (1965): pp. 10-13.

Cappick, Marie. "Streets," *Coral Tribune* (November 1, 1957).

Cutter, Bowman. "Architecture of Towers, *The Martello Towers and the Story of Key West* (1953): pp. 12-13.

Cutter, Bowman, and Colin Jameson. "Architecture of the Martello Towers," *The Martello Towers and the Story of Key West* (1953): pp. 17-18.

Florida Keys and Land Trust. "The Salt Ponds of Key West."

References

Jameson, Colin. "Key West's Old Ironsides," *The Martello Towers and the Story of Key West* (1953): pp.14-15.

Jameson, Colin. "What's in a Street Name?" Florida Collection 29, Monroe County Public Library: pp. 26-30.

Smiley, Nora. "Four Founding Fathers," *Martello*, no. 5 (1968): pp. 5-6.

Wells, Sharon. *Walking and Birding Guide to Key West*, vol. XV (1998).

Fiction Bibliography

Most of the quotes inserted in the text were borrowed from the following:

Corcoran, Tom. *The Mango Opera*. New York: St. Martin's Paperbacks, 1998.

-----. *Gumbo Limbo*. New York: St. Martin's Paperbacks, 1999.

-----. *Bone Island Mambo*. New York: St. Martin's Paperbacks, 2001.

-----. *Octopus Alibi*. New York: St. Martin's Press, 2003.

Francis, Dorothy. *Conch Shell Murder*. Chandler, Arizona: Five Star Publications, 2003.

Hall, James W. *Bones of Coral*. New York: Dell Publishing, 1991.

-----. *Red Sky at Night*. New York: Dell Publishing, 1997.

Harrison, Jim. *A Good Day to Die*. New York: Dell Publishing, 1973.

Hemingway, Ernest. *To Have and Have Not*. London: Grafton Books, 1972.

Hersey, John. *Key West Tales*. New York: Vintage Books, 1993.

Fiction Bibliography

Hirschfeld, Burt. *Key West*. New York: Golden Apple Publishers, 1978.

Leslie, John. *Blood on the Keys*. New York: Pocket Books, 1988.

-----. *Killer in Paradise*. New York: Pocket Books, 1990.

-----. *Damaged Goods*. New York: Pocket Books, 1993.

-----. *Killing Me Softly*. New York: Pocket Books, 1994.

Lurie, Alison. *The Truth About Lorin Jones*. Boston: Little, Brown and Company, 1988.

-----. *The Last Resort*. New York: Henry Holt and Company, 1998.

Macomber, Robert N. *Point of Honor*. Sarasota, Florida: Pineapple Press, 2003.

McGuane, Thomas. *Panama*. New York: Penguin Books, 1979.

-----. *Ninety-two in the Shade*. New York: Penguin Books, 1980.

-----. *The Bushwhacked Piano*. New York: Vintage Books, 1984.

Sanchez, Thomas. *Mile Zero*. New York: Vintage Books, 1990.

Shames, Laurence. *Florida Straits*. New York: Dell Publishing, 1993.

Shames, Laurence. *Sunburn*. New York: Hyperion, 1995.

-----. *Tropical Depression*. New York: Hyperion, 1996.

-----. *Virgin Heat*. New York: Hyperion, 1997.

Strabel, Thelma. *Reap the Wild Wind*. New York: Triangle Book, 1943.

Woods, Stuart. *Choke*. New York: HarperPaperbacks, 1996.

Index

Index

Index

If you enjoyed reading this book, here are some other Pineapple Press titles you might enjoy as well. To request our complete catalog or to place an order, write to Pineapple Press, P.O. Box 3889, Sarasota, Florida 34230, or call 1-800-PINEAPL (746-3275). Or visit our website at www.pineapplepress.com.

The Florida Keys Volume 1: *A History of the Pioneers* by John Viele. As recently as 80 years ago, fewer than 300 inhabitants tried to eke out a living without electricity, running water, radios, or telephones in the subtropical heat of the Florida Keys. As vividly portrayed as if they were characters in a novel, the true-life inhabitants of the Keys will capture your admiration as you share in the dreams and realities of their daily lives. ISBN 1-56164-101-4 (hb)

The Florida Keys Volume 2: *True Stories of the Perilous Straits* by John Viele. Thousands of people have died in shipwrecks, attacks by natives, sea battles, and pirate boardings along the treacherous Straits of Florida. Excerpted from ships' logs, captains' diaries, court-martial transcripts, and newspaper accounts, here's a selection of gripping stories during the age of sail from the time Spanish navigators discovered the straits to the end of the Second Seminole War in 1842. ISBN 1-56164-179-0 (hb)

The Florida Keys Volume 3: *The Wreckers* by John Viele. Culled from various sources, these true stories capture the drama of the lives and times of the Florida Keys wreckers, those daring seamen who sailed out in weather fair or foul to save lives and property from ships cast up on the unforgiving Florida Reef. ISBN 1-56164-219-3 (hb)

The Florida Chronicles by Stuart B. McIver. A series offering true-life sagas of the notable and notorious characters throughout history who have given Florida its distinctive flavor. **Volume 1** *Dreamers, Schemers and Scalawags* ISBN 1-56164-155-3 (pb); **Volume 2** *Murder in the Tropics* ISBN 1-56164-079-4 (hb); **Volume 3** *Touched by the Sun* ISBN 1-56164-206-1 (hb)

Key Biscayne by Joan Gill Blank. This engaging history of the southernmost barrier island in the U.S. tells the stories of its owners and would-be owners. ISBN 1-56164-096-4 (hb); 1-56164-103-0 (pb)

Key West Gardens and Their Stories by Janis Frawley-Holler. Sneak a peek into the lush, tropical gardens of old Key West. Enjoy beautiful views of the islanders' sanctuaries as well as fascinating stories and histories of the grounds where gardens now grow. ISBN 1-56164-204-5 (pb)